JUMP START TO

C PROGRAMMING
&
_{THE} UNIX INTERFACE

JUMP START TO

C PROGRAMMING
&
THE UNIX INTERFACE

Derek Kiong Beng Kee
National University of Singapore

PRENTICE HALL
Singapore   New York   London   Toronto   Sydney   Tokyo

First published 1995 by
Prentice Hall
Simon & Schuster (Asia) Pte Ltd
Alexandra Distripark
Block 4, #04-31
Pasir Panjang Road
Singapore 0511

UNIX and Solaris are trademarks of Novell and Sun Microsystems respectively.

Printed in Singapore

1 2 3 4 5   99 98 97 96 95

ISBN 981-3026-66-9

Prentice Hall International (UK) Limited, *London*
Prentice Hall of Australia Pty. Limited, *Sydney*
Prentice Hall Canada Inc., *Toronto*
Prentice Hall Hispanoamericana, S.A., *Mexico*
Prentice Hall of India Private Limited, *New Delhi*
Prentice Hall of Japan, Inc., *Tokyo*
Editora Prentice Hall do Brasil, Ltda., *Rio de Janeiro*
Prentice Hall, Inc., *Englewood Cliffs, New Jersey*

*For Mum and Dad, who provided countless opportunities
to explore why things work the way they do.*

Contents

1   Introduction 1

    1. 1   Von Neumann Machines 2
    1. 2   Using High-level Languages 3
    1. 3   An Abstract View of C 5
    1. 4   Comparison with Pascal 6
    1. 5   Summary 9

2   A Quick Tour of C 11

    2. 1   Browser Overview 11
    2. 2   Library Interface Information 12
    2. 3   File Representation 12
    2. 4   Navigation Through the File 15
    2. 5   Displaying File Contents 17
    2. 6   Reading Files 18
    2. 7   Interpreting User Requests 20
    2. 8   Initialising the Browser 21
    2. 9   Improvements to the Browser 22
    2. 10 Summary 22
    2. 11 Exercises 23

3   The Run-time Organisation of C Programs 25

    3. 1   Program Compilation 25
    3. 2   Run-time Organisation of a Program 26
    3. 3   Allocation of Heap Storage 28
    3. 4   Pointer Indirection 29
    3. 5   Legitimate Memory Access 30
    3. 6   Modular Structure 33

3. 7   Libraries 37
3. 8   Preprocessor Directives 38
3. 9   Function `main()` and Program Parameters 41
3. 10 Summary 42
3. 11 Exercises 43

4   Using *curses* for Interactive Applications **45**

4. 1   Objectives of *termcap* and *curses* Libraries 45
4. 2   A Basic I/O Interface for Interactive Applications 47
4. 3   Improving the File Browser 50
4. 4   Linking Object Modules with Libraries 53
4. 5   Other *curses* Features 54
4. 6   Summary 58
4. 7   Exercises 59

5   C Syntax and Semantics **61**

5. 1   Definitions 61
5. 2   Variable Definitions 62
5. 3   Structured Variables 62
5. 4   Declarators 64
5. 5   Type Declarations 68
5. 6   Statements and Expressions 68
5. 7   Control-flow Constructs 74
5. 8   Function Definitions 78
5. 9   Parameter Passing 79
5. 10 Type Casting 81
5. 11 Storage-class Specifiers 82
5. 12 Independent Compilation 84
5. 13 Summary 84
5. 14 Exercises 84

6   Making System Calls **87**

6. 1   Notation and Documentation 88
6. 2   Making a System Call 89
6. 3   Error Codes and Error Reporting 90
6. 4   Summary 91

7   File Manipulation **93**

7. 1   Reading and Writing Files 94
7. 2   Non-sequence File Access 100
7. 3   Directory Operations 101
7. 4   File Links 103
7. 5   File Attributes 105

7. 6   Buffering Input/Output Operations 107
7. 7   *stdio* Library Package 108
7. 8   Mixing *stdio* Operations with System Calls 116
7. 9   Summary 117
7. 10 Exercises 118

8   UNIX Processes **119**

8. 1   The Process Environment 120
8. 2   Spawning a New Process 121
8. 3   Executing Another Program 124
8. 4   Input/Output Redirection 127
8. 5   Basic Interprocess Communication 130
8. 6   Process Characteristics 134
8. 7   *setuid* Programs 136
8. 8   Changing User and Group IDs 137
8. 9   Summary 139
8. 10 Exercises 140

9   Administrative Information **141**

9. 1   User Account Information 141
9. 2   Passwords and Password Encryption 144
9. 3   Time Functions 146
9. 4   Using Temporary Files 148
9. 5   Using Environment Variables 149
9. 6   Summary 149
9. 7   Exercises 150

10 Signals and Exceptions **151**

10. 1 Sending Signals to Processes 152
10. 2 Responding to a Signal 155
10. 3 The Role of Signal Handlers 158
10. 4 Exceptions 158
10. 5 Non-local Branches from Signal Handlers 161
10. 6 Implementing Timeouts 163
10. 7 Signals and Re-entrant Code 165
10. 8 Summary 165
10. 9 Exercises 166

11 Handling Terminals **167**

11. 1 Terminal Line Overview 168
11. 2 Reading and Setting Terminal-device Characteristics 169
11. 3 Interpreting and Operating on `termios` Fields 171
11. 4 Key Bindings for Special Characters 175

11. 5   Local Modes 177
11. 6   Input Modes 178
11. 7   Output Modes 179
11. 8   Hardware Control Modes 180
11. 9   Using Non-Canonical Input Mode 181
11. 10 Summary 185
11. 11 Exercises 185

Appendix UNIX Programming Tools **187**
A. 1   vi for File Editing and More 187
A. 2   ctags for Generating C Tags File 190
A. 3   The gcc Compiler 191
A. 4   make to Make Up-to-date Versions 193
A. 5   The gdb Debugger 197
A. 6   The prof Profiler 201
A. 7   The gprof Profiler 203
A. 8   Summary 205

Bibliography **207**

Index **209**

Preface

The course IC173 "UNIX tools and C Programming" is a new undergraduate module offered by the Department of Information Systems and Computer Science, National University of Singapore. The main focus of the course is to provide a comprehensive introduction to the UNIX environment and the C programming language. Many in the industry regard C as a practical language for two reasons: the language has proven itself, having been used to build significant portions of the UNIX operating system, and more recently, it has been successfully used in the building of many applications.

This book is written as an introductory text to using C and UNIX for software development. It builds on the reader's knowledge of Pascal so that programming exercises can be started quickly.

It would be insufficient for computer science majors to know just C syntax or semantics, operating commands, or shell programming. These would only skim the surface. An understanding of the implementation aspects of C and UNIX implies familiarity with the semantics of C and an appreciation for the pragmatic use of the language. In the face of program errors, knowledge of the run-time environment allows symptoms to be analysed systematically to provide appropriate deductions about program behaviour.

A good understanding of the key mechanisms in UNIX also provides a foundation for more thorough exploration and reasoning about programming languages and their implementations. It is useful in systems programming and other software development related efforts. This provides in turn the opportunity to relate material covered in other computer science courses, such as the design and implementation of operating systems, compilers and computer architecture.

The skills to be acquired are thus more fundamental than just learning to write computer programs. The objective of this book is to provide the reader with a quick but thorough start to learning the C programming language, its run-time environment and software development in the UNIX environment.

Learning C programming is easier with some knowledge and practice of programming in another language, such as Pascal. We build upon this foundation to explore C, which is a different language, but with a similar programming paradigm, namely procedural or imperative programming. The origins of the C programming language are closely related with the UNIX operating system. As such, our discussion will include the relevant parts of the UNIX operating system, such as the operating system interface and standard libraries. In addition, UNIX contains many useful programming tools. The essential ones relating to writing C programs will be discussed in the appendix. The hope is that readers will be encouraged to investigate the use of other tools too.

UNIX has a gradual learning curve. This could be due to it being originally designed for programmers. Investigation is often hindered by the daunting nature of manuals and a lack of understanding of the UNIX philosophy. This document will attempt to address these issues, and provide a foundation for readers to build modest UNIX applications. We hope that the satisfaction gained from such development efforts will lead to further exploration of the more advanced features documented in the standard UNIX manuals.

An adventurous and dauntless attitude will pave the way to learning about program development in a UNIX environment. These qualities are often found in the souls of UNIX programmers.

Overview

Chapter 1 focuses on the similarities of the Pascal and C programming languages. Both have a programming paradigm based on the Von Neuman machine. Chapter 2 provides a quick tour of C by using a simple and crude file browser program. The browser in this case study will gradually be refined over subsequent chapters when more mechanisms of C and UNIX are reviewed.

Chapter 3 discusses some issues related to the implementation of C. This includes the mapping of C constructs to machine code and run-time characteristics. A better insight of how C constructs are ultimately implemented provides a good understanding of the language semantics and the common pitfalls to be avoided.

Chapter 4 gives insights into how the *curses* library may be used. The facilities found here are used to improve the browser developed in the previous chapter. It also gives a clearer picture of program development in the UNIX environment.

Having thus provided sufficient exposure to C programs, chapter 5 gives a more detailed account of the mechanisms available. Following that, an introduction to how UNIX system calls might be used is presented in chapter 6.

The system calls that operate on the file system are discussed in chapter 7. Since *stdio* routines are often used, they are also reviewed and contrasted with equivalent system calls.

Chapter 8 discusses the system calls relating to the process environment in UNIX. It will show how new processes may be created. Related issues on how programs are loaded, how pipes might be used for simple interprocess communication, and the execution of privileged programs are also discussed.

Chapter 9 looks at the password file and the user information it contains. Details of how passwords are encrypted, miscellaneous routines, such as time format conversions, temporary files and environment symbols are also discussed.

Many non-trivial programs also require the use of UNIX signals and manipulate characteristics of terminals. Chapters 10 and 11 provide an overview of these aspects. Finally, the appendix closes with the standard program development tools available in the UNIX environment.

Readers are encouraged to explore features discussed in greater detail. Additional references are provided in the summary sections. In most cases, the discussion is applicable to any generic version of UNIX. The version of UNIX used for this course is Solaris 2.3. Where there is variation, the discussion will apply only to this version.

Code fragments may be obtained via *WEB* clients such as *LYNX*, *MOSAIC* and *NETSCAPE* at the URL `http://www.iscs.nus.sg/~dkiong/jumpStart`.

Acknowledgments

I am thankful to colleagues at the Department of Information Systems and Computer Science, National University of Singapore for their encouragement and suggestions. I am deeply indebted to Professor Ling Tok Wang for having sufficient faith in me to teach this course, and the Dean of the Science Faculty for allowing this text to be used. If not for these decisions, this text would probably not have been written.

I am also thankful for the use of the computing resource at my work place. The machines, network, modems and laser printers have made this task less painful.

Ms Lim Eng Lian read the very early drafts and suggested how I might proceed. Dr John McCallum read later drafts and provided more suggestions. Due to tight schedules, I take the blame for being unable to incorporate all of them. Many thanks also to staff from Prentice Hall. They have been helpful, patient and yet efficient in getting this text published quickly.

Derek Kiong Beng Kee
July 1995

1

Introduction

A quick way for Pascal programmers to learn C is to understand the similarities between the two languages. It is also useful to appreciate that both are based on the same computational model. The programming languages C and Pascal are closely related in that both are imperative languages. They both allow the specification of a sequence of tasks that compute and move values amongst a set of variables. The Pascal function in Figure 1-1 to compute factorial illustrates this model:

```
function factorial(n:integer):integer;
   var result:integer;
   begin
      result:=1;
      while (n <> 1) do begin
         result:=result*n;
         n:=n-1
      end;
      factorial:=result
   end;
```

Figure 1-1: factorial function in Pascal

An initial value is first assigned to the local variable result. It is updated at each iteration in the loop so that its intermediate value approaches the intended result. In addition, the counter n is decremented so that the loop is executed n times.

An imperative program describes **how** a result is obtained, but not necessarily **what** is obtained. This computation model resembles the workings of traditional Von Neumann computing machines, upon which such languages are based and implemented.

For a quick comparison, an equivalent factorial function in C is shown in Figure 1-2.

```
int factorial(int n)
{
    int result;

    result = 1;
    while (n != 1) {
        result = result*n;
        n--;
    }
    return(result);
}
```

Figure 1-2: factorial function in C

1. 1   Von Neumann Machines

A computing machine based on the traditional Von Neumann model consists of CPU and memory units. The CPU operates sequentially by fetching an instruction from memory, and interpreting each in turn. An instruction might involve

- moving a value in a memory location or register to a suitable destination,

- computing a new value by operating on existing values,

- testing the status of a value, or

- transferring control to a new address location from which to fetch the next instruction for execution.

Other than a transfer of control, instructions are normally executed sequentially until some state is obtained. The terminating condition is one determined by the programmer, as specified in the program.

Similarly, a Pascal program may be viewed as consisting of variable definitions and code statements to:

- assign values to variables via assignment statements,

- compute new values via expressions, and

- modify the sequential flow of execution via structured control flow constructs.

Variable definitions provide the functionality of memory cells that store intermediate results. This illustrates the importance of abstractions in high-level languages. Although machine details such as addresses and storage requirements of variables with the appropriate allocation and deallocation strategies are important, they are not the main concern of the high-level language programmer. Instead such details are deferred and maintained by the language implementation. This is the chief purpose of high-level languages: to allow programmers to concentrate on algorithm and design concerns. Mundane machine details are secondary, and much better considered separately by the compiler.

Similarly, expressions in a high-level language specify what is to be computed. The compiler generates appropriate code to compute the intended value, using registers or temporary memory locations as necessary for intermediate values. In addition, structured statements specify control flow in a program without concern for label names, addresses or branch destinations.

Both variables and code must be loaded and represented appropriately in a "Pascal machine" before execution in accordance with the semantics of the language can proceed. When program execution is started, the code specifies what values are to be computed and moved amongst various variable locations. Execution proceeds until the desired state is attained, which presumably is after the last statement.

An actual Pascal machine is typically implemented via software. It takes the form of a Pascal compiler which translates Pascal code into native machine code. This enables program execution on a traditional Von Neumann machine. Each variable is mapped onto a suitable location in the memory of the target machine. The resultant machine instructions then manipulate values by accessing appropriate memory locations which correspond to such high-level variables.

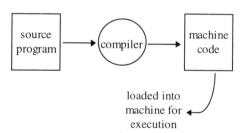

Figure 1-3: Compiler input and output

1. 2   Using High-level Languages

While the programming model of high-level languages like Pascal and C are similar to that of Von Neumann computing machines, they are different in that higher-level mechanisms are incorporated which allow for easy code specification. Such abstractions are also less error-prone. Some of these facilities include:

- the use of expressions involving standard mathematical notations,

- data-structuring facilities such as record and array types,

- structured control constructs such as loop and conditional statements, and

- code abstraction facilities such as functions with parameter-passing mechanisms.

While some techniques may also be adopted in assembly language, a high-level language supports them consistently.

Even though the high-level mechanisms provided by different languages may vary, the task of learning a new programming language is made easier by relying on mechanisms already understood in the cousin language. In this case, it is easy for a Pascal programmer to learn C because many of the high-level mechanisms of C are already found in Pascal. The significant difference between the two is that a function declaration in C may not be nested in another function. As such, the Pascal style and conventions for scoping program entities do not always apply when programming in C.

The C programming language was also designed to enable the implementation of parts of the UNIX operating system. Currently, the complete operating system, except for the kernel, is implemented in C. The design rationale of C was a compromise between being sufficiently high level so that design logic may be inferred from code, and sufficiently low level to allow machine-specific details to be manipulated. Thus, C does not include very high-level abstractions which may be expensive to implement. Instead, sufficient language primitives are available to allow the implementation of other facilities which the programmer might require.

Pascal has been designed with appropriate restrictions so that mistakes are more difficult to make. Where a mistake is made, there are sufficient safeguards for it to be detected. On the other hand, the language facilities and restrictions offered in C are minimal. They are however highly amenable for translation to machine code as it is to be used for systems programming. Curbing the flexibility of the language is viewed as restrictive and unnecessary for experienced programmers. Novice C programmers consequently find it easier to make mistakes which are more difficult to discover and correct. However, this is partly caused by an insufficient understanding of the run-time behaviour of programs. In this respect, knowledge of how C is implemented, as explained in chapter 3, will help.

Finally, a practical software development language must support independent compilation. This feature has enabled the C language proper to be small, but with a large and varied set of libraries. In fact, C does not even define any input/output facilities. Instead, a major bulk of input and output operations required has been implemented in the standard input/output (*stdio*) library. Several such library routines and appropriate system calls are reviewed in chapter 7.

1. 3   An Abstract View of C

As with all imperative languages, Pascal and C are reliant on variables. Values of variables in C are typically set via an assignment operator. This has the same effect as a MOV instruction in assembly code. As with Pascal, expressions allow arithmetic operations to be specified naturally. The language compiler translates such code to appropriate machine instructions which make use of temporary locations for intermediate results.

User-defined type definitions allow appropriate data structures to model the real world problem domain. The storage requirements of such composite types may exceed those of predefined types. The compiler must determine the storage requirements of such aggregate types and perform appropriate allocations and deallocations. An assignment operator must then generate code to copy an appropriate number of bytes corresponding to the storage allocation. These are the benefits of the abstraction features available in high-level languages.

Structured control constructs such as conditional and loop statements allow other more basic statements to be executed selectively or repetitively. In this aspect, the while loop and if-else statements in C are similar to those of Pascal. Furthermore, the switch statement in C is also quite similar to the case statement of Pascal. Minor differences in semantics do not detract from the fact that such control abstracts relieve the programmer from concern with label sites and branch destinations. An assembly language programmer in comparison must remember all label sites so as to implement appropriate control flow. Unfortunately, attention to design logic is often diverted to concern over these implementation details.

Finally, procedural abstraction mechanisms allow programmers to solve a problem in manageable increments. This might be compared to building complementing sub-machines and combining them to form a complete solution. C functions support the task of stepwise refinement, as well as the opportunity for reusing in possibly different contexts. A flexible parameter-passing mechanism helps meet the latter requirement. While Pascal differentiates between procedures and functions, C only provides the more general form of function definitions. Procedures are merely functions that do not return any value.

As mentioned earlier, function definitions in C may only occur at the global top level, unlike a nested sub-program hierarchy as in Pascal. Since C adopts static scoping conventions, C functions may only access two kinds of variables: global variables and its own local variables.

By default, global variables and function definitions are compiled into public names for the linker. This feature allows code in an object module to access variables or invoke functions defined in a different program file. It is this feature which facilitates independent compilation, and will be discussed at greater length in chapter 3.

1. 4   Comparison with Pascal

Table 1-1 provides a summary of the facilities available in C, together with a short description of the semantics. Where appropriate, Pascal equivalents are shown for easy comparison. Details of each facility will be further elaborated on in chapter 5.

C construct	Pascal equivalent	Remarks
literal symbols:		
`123`	`123`	decimal literal
`0123`	`n.a.`[1]	octal literal (begins with 0)
`3.4`	`3.4`	floating point literal
`'a'`	`'a'`	character literal
`'\n'`	`n.a.`	special character (newline)
`'\015'`	`n.a.`	char by ASCII octal value
`"abcde"`	`'abcde'`	string literal
`0 1`	`false   true`	boolean values
definitions:		
`int a;`	`a:integer;`	integer variable
`char b;`	`b:char;`	character variable
`float c;`	`c:real;`	floating point variable
`char *d;`	`d:^char;`	pointer variable to char
`char e[10];`	`e:array[0..9]of char;`	character array variable
`char **f;`	`f:^^char;`	pointer-to-pointer variable
`int (*g)();`	`n.a.`	pointer-to-function variable
`char *h[10];`	`h:array[0..9]of ^char;`	array of pointers variable
`char i[10][5];`	`h:array[0..9,0..4]of char;`	two-dimensional array variable

`struct r {`
`   int f1;`
`   char *f2;`
`};`
	`type r = record`
	`            f1:integer;`
	`            f2:^char;`
	`          end;`
		record type

`union u {`
`   int f3;`
`   float f4;`
`};`
	`u = record case int of`
	`        1:(f3:integer);`
	`        2:(f4:real);`
	`      end;`
		union type

`struct r v;`	`var v:r;`	record variable
`struct r w[5];`	`w:array[0..4] of r;`	array of records variable
`struct r *p;`	`p:^r;`	pointer-to-record variable

---

[1]   n.a. = not available

C construct	Pascal equivalent	Remarks

`t f(int i)`
`{ `*`local-definitions`*
`   `*`statements`*
`}`
	`function f(i:integer):t;`
	`local-definitions`
	`begin`
	`   `*`statement`*
	`end;`
		function definition
		(procedure is a function which returns a `void` value)

operators:		
`+ - * /` `%`	`+ - * div /` `mod`	arithmetic operators (C performs integer division on integers)

`== !=`
`>  >=`
`<  <=`
	`=  <>`
	`>  >=`
	`<  <=`
		equality/inequality tests
		relational tests

`&&  ||  !`	`and  or  not`	logical operators (C operators are short-circuit)
`&	~`	n.a.	bitwise and/or/complement
expressions:		
`*x`	`x^`	pointer indirection
`&x`	n.a.	unary address-of operator
`x[i]`	`x[i]`	array subscript
`v.f1` `p->f1`	`v.f1` `p^.f1`	field access
`f(expn`$_1$`, ...expn`$_k$`)` `f()`	`f(expn`$_1$`, ...expn`$_k$`)` `f`	function call with k params call with no parameters
`c ? a : b`	n.a.	if `c <> 0` result is `a` else `b`
side-effect:		
`=`	`:=`	assignment operator
`x `*`op=`*` y` `x += y`	n.a.	$x := x\ op\ y$ $x := x + y$

`++x`
`x++`
`--x`
`x--`
	n.a.	prefix increment
		postfix increment
		prefix decrement
		postfix decrement
		prefix (postfix) increment returns `x` after (before) the increment

`*x++`	n.a.	pointer indirection on the result of postfix increment on `x`
statements:		
`{ s1;s2;s3; }`	`begin s1;s2;s3 end`	statement sequence **;** terminates C statement
`if (exp) s;`	`if exp<>0 then s;`	conditional statement

C construct	Pascal equivalent	Remarks
`if (exp) s1;` `else s2;`	`if exp<>0 then s1 else s2;`	two-way conditional statement

`switch (exp) {`
`   case k:s;`
`         break;`
`   ...`
`}`
	`case exp of`
	`   k:s;`
	`   ...`
	`end;`
		multi-way alternative

`while (exp) s;`	`while exp<>0 do s;`	pre-test iteration
`do s; while (exp);`	`repeat s until exp=0;`	post-test iteration

`for (s1;exp;s2) s3;`	`s1; while exp<>0 do begin`
	`   s3; s2`
	`end;`
		template for pre-test iteration

`return(exp);`
 	
`return;`
	n.a.	return from function with `exp` result
		return, but with no result

`continue;`	n.a.	stop current iteration
`break;`	n.a.	break out from loop
miscellaneous:		
`sizeof(x)`	n.a.	return size of object `x`
`(type) exp`	n.a.	changing the type of `exp` by type casting
source pre-processing:		
`/* comments */`	`(* ... *)   { ... }`	comment conventions

`#define M w`
 	
`#define M(x) w`
	n.a.	replace occurrences of `M` with `w` before compilation.
		parameterized substitution

`#ifdef A`
`   X`
`#endif`
`#if B`
`   Y`
`#endif`
	n.a.	conditional compilation:
		`X` is compiled if `A` is defined
		
		`Y` is compiled if `B` evaluates to non zero

`#else` `#ifndef`	n.a.	conditional compilation: may be used with `#else` and `#ifndef` (if not defined)
`#include "f"` `#include <g>`	n.a.	source file inclusion: `f` is relative to current directory `g` is relative to system `#include` directory

Table 1-1: Quick summary of language facilities in C

1. 5 **Summary**

The following points were discussed in this chapter:

§   Assembler, Pascal and C are procedural languages.

§   The computational model of procedural languages relies on moving values amongst memory cells or variables, sequential execution and occasional condition tests with possible control flow branches.

§   Abstraction facilities offered by high-level languages hide machine details from programmers.

§   While C and Pascal differ in syntax, they have similar program structures, and much of C can be understood in terms of Pascal.

Subsequent chapters will provide more details of mechanisms available in C and the UNIX environment.

2

A Quick Tour of C

This chapter presents a quick tour of the C programming language by using a simple and crude file browser program. Its features will be gradually refined when more mechanisms of C and UNIX are reviewed in subsequent chapters.

2. 1   Browser Overview

A typical file browser program must allow users to conveniently view the contents of a file. The main concerns would be to implement suitable display and traversal facilities. Since the contents of most files cannot be displayed on a 24-line screen of a typical terminal, users must be content with viewing only various portions of the file. A simple traversal facility (possibly via scrolling) may be employed to make the relevant portions visible.

A browser program may be seen as consisting of the following components:

- a file representation data structure which is created when file contents are read during browser initialisation,

- a navigation mechanism for moving through the above representation and selecting portions of interest,

- a screen display mechanism that allows a selected file region to be viewed, and

- a command interpreter to read and interpret user's navigation requests.

2. 2   Library Interface Information

Reading and displaying file contents, and reading user commands from the keyboard require the standard input/output library package. The associated interface information is included from the file stdio.h. Similarly, information about the C standard library functions are found in the file stdlib.h. The preprocessor directive #include instructs the compiler to read the specified file at compile time.

```
#include <stdio.h>
#include <stdlib.h>
```

A .h header file contains details of entities made available by the library. Such entities may be symbolic constants, function prototypes or external variable declarations. The actual file contents are typically not easily readable since they are meant for the C compiler. The human-readable information is found in UNIX man pages.

2. 3   File Representation

Data structures for file representation may be simplified if the complete file is read in at initialisation time. The more efficient scenario is where portions of the input file are read only when displaying the associated context, as this conserves memory requirements. However, this approach is not to be considered because of the resulting additional complexity. Since the browser program is for illustration, we will use the simpler representation. We are thus restricted to browsing files which are sufficiently small to comfortably fit into the data space of a process.

File contents are organised into lines so that additional processing for display purposes is not required. However, the number of lines in each file and the number of characters in each line cannot be assumed. This situation calls for a standard doubly-linked list of lines. Each line representation also references a memory block sufficiently large to hold characters of that line. Memory allocation is thus performed at run time since memory requirements will only be known after each line is read and its length known. Furthermore, the total number of lines in the file is only known after reading the last line.

The following Line record structure is used to represent a line and comprises three fields. The contents field references (or contains the address of) the memory block for characters of that line. The previous and next fields reference the Line structure of the previous and next lines respectively. The exceptions would be the instances corresponding to the first and last lines when the respective previous and next fields would both be NULL. This NULL value is the same as the Pascal nil value which indicates that a pointer does not reference any object.

```
struct Line {
  char *contents;
  struct Line *previous, *next;
};
```

The file representation is graphically illustrated in Figure 2-1.

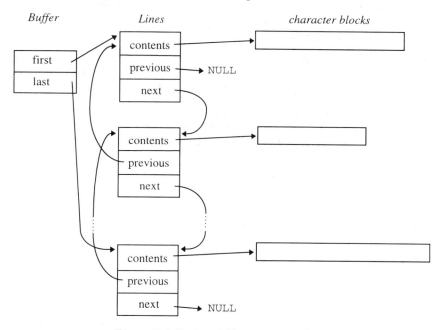

Figure 2-1: Internal file representation

We represent file contents by using a `Buffer` structure consisting of references to the first and last instances of the `Line` structure.

```
struct Buffer {
  struct Line *first, *last;
};
```

We declare `text` as a `Buffer` variable, with both its fields initialised to `NULL`.

```
struct Buffer text = { NULL, NULL };
```

Variable and field definitions in C serve the same purpose as those in Pascal: they state the properties of the entity and bind them to the specified types so that subsequent operations on the entity may be checked for type compatibility. As mentioned previously, the compiler calculates storage requirements and performs appropriate allocations.

Note the differences in the concrete syntax for definitions. It is unlike Pascal because the type specifier precedes the name of the entity. Furthermore, an asterisk "*" precedes a pointer variable. For convenience, a variable definition in C, such as text, may include an initial value determined at compile time.

Each input line is appended to the doubly-linked list via the function append(). Briefly, it must allocate storage for a new instance of Line and perform the appropriate pointer manipulation to initialise a list or append it to the existing list.

The representation of character strings is discussed in the next chapter. For the moment, it would suffice to refer to a string by the address of its first byte. The formal parameter linechars is thus the address of a character.

```c
void append(char *linechars)
{
  struct Line *ln;

  ln = malloc(sizeof(struct Line));
  if (ln == NULL) {
    printf("insufficient heap memory\n");
    exit(1);
  }
  if (text.first == NULL) {                /* inserting the first line */
    text.first = ln;
    ln->next = ln->previous = NULL;
  } else {                        /* appending to last line via text.last */
    text.last->next = ln;
    ln->previous = text.last;
    ln->next = NULL;
  }
  text.last = ln;
  ln->contents = linechars;
}
```

Even if the concrete syntax for function definitions in C differ from those in Pascal, it should be recognised that in abstract terms, they do not differ. A function definition still consists of the function name, parameter names and associated types, result type and the function body proper which specifies the implementation part. linechars is a formal parameter and ln is a local variable. Their associated types are char pointer and struct Line pointer. Just as with the type of a variable, the type of the return result precedes the function name. In this case, void denotes none. Instead, it specifies a procedure.

Local variables may be declared within blocks, denoted by curly braces. While blocks in Pascal only appear as function or procedure bodies, blocks in C may also be statement parts.

Since `ln` is a pointer variable to `struct Line` items, it is assigned the address of a `struct Line` object. The storage for the latter is allocated at run time because the number of lines is unknown at compile time. Such dynamic allocation is performed explicitly via a call to `malloc()` with the amount of bytes required. When the request is successful, it returns the address of the allocated block. This implies that `malloc()` will not reassign the area for a different purpose, thus leading to inconsistency.

The function `sizeof()` returns the storage requirements of a type, or storage allocation of a variable. As types and variables are all analysed at compile time, the function `sizeof()` is merely a compile-time function. Since the heap manager `malloc()` returns `NULL` when it cannot fulfill an allocation request, we confirm that it has not happened. If it had, we would be unable to proceed, and would thus abort execution via `exit()` to terminate the program.

Although the difference between the syntax for assignment "=" and equality "==" operators is minor, it is very important due to the drastic difference in semantics. Additionally, the semantics of the assignment in C is slightly different from those of Pascal, in that it returns the assigned value. Thus, as seen in the function `append()`, it may be involved in another assignment.

Strings in C are delimited by double quotes ("). The newline character is not represented literally since that would complicate the case when the closing delimiter is missing. The unique notation "\n" is used instead. In the simplest case, `printf()` outputs strings.

While it was mentioned earlier that "*" precedes pointer values, it is more accurate to say that "*" is the prefix indirection operator. In this case of `*ln`, the "*" operator returns the variable of type `struct Line` addressed by the pointer (or address value of) `ln`. In this aspect, the "*" indirection operator is similar to "^" in Pascal.

Since the field selector operator is ".", `(*ln).contents` references the contents of the line pointed to by the pointer variable `ln`. This may be shortened, as in the last assignment in the function `append()`, to the equivalent notation `ln->contents`.

2. 4   Navigation Through the File

For navigation purposes, another pointer variable `current` is used to reference the current line of focus. Commands to move to the next or previous text screen would update this pointer. In effect, it maintains the state of navigating through the file contents. The integer variable `lineNumber` maintains the corresponding line number.

```
struct Line *current;
int lineNumber;
```

Since it is logical to start browsing from the first line, these variables will be set to address the first line during initialisation.

```
void home()
{
  current = text.first;
  lineNumber = 1;
}
```

Scrolling forward and backward involve traversing through n lines. However, precautions must be taken so as not to proceed past the first or last lines when scrolling backward or forward respectively.

```
void forward(int n)
{
  while (n-- && (current != text.last)) {
    current = current->next;
    lineNumber++;
  }
}

void backward(int n)
{
  while (n-- && (current != text.first)) {
    current = current->previous;
    lineNumber--;
  }
}
```

The semantics of the if conditional and pre-test while loop constructs in C is similar to those in Pascal. However, C does not provide a predefined boolean type. A zero value denotes a *false* boolean value, while all other (non-zero) values denote a *true* boolean value.

The notation for the inequality operator is "!=", while that for the logical AND and OR operators are "&&" and "||" respectively.

For execution efficiency, C provides both prefix and postfix increment ++ and decrement -- operators. The postfix decrement operator in functions backward() and forward() decrements n but returns the operand's original value. The associated effect is that the loop is executed n times, for as long as the first or last lines have not been encountered.

Since parameters are passed by value, the value n is independent of that of the original actual parameter, and modifying n does not affect the original parameter.

2. 5   Displaying File Contents

To display a screenful of file contents, m lines starting from the current line current are printed, m being dependent on the screen height. Blank lines are added if there are less than m lines in the context. This ensures that the previous display will be scrolled off the screen.

```
void display(int m)
{
   int lineNum = lineNumber;
   struct Line *display = current;

   do {
      printf("%4d    %s\n", lineNum++, display->contents);
      display = display->next;
      m--;
   } while ((display != NULL) && (m != 0));
   while (m--)
      printf("\n");
}
```

Unlike the while construct, the do construct is a post-test iterative construct. Its body is executed at least once, just like the repeat loop in Pascal. This is consistent with our display requirements since the current pointer variable will always reference a line in the buffer, and we would like to display at least one line.

While the library routine printf() has been used to output a character string, it is actually more flexible in allowing formatted output. The first parameter specifies the conversion and format in which subsequent parameters should be printed. In this case, "%4d" and "%s" are conversion specifications which mean a decimal number (of length four) and a string respectively. The expressions lineNum++ and display->contents are to be converted and extrapolated into the original format specification which specifies three spaces between the line number and line contents.

Note that the logical operators "&&" and "||" in C perform partial evaluation. Where the first operand of the AND && operator is false, that result may be returned without evaluating the second operand. Similarly, where the first operand of the OR || operator is true, that result may be returned without evaluating the second operand. Thus, the following fragment would differ from the original because --m is not executed when the value of the sub-expression (display != NULL) is false:

```
do {
   printf("%4d    %s\n", lineNum++, display->contents);
   display = display->next;
} while ((display != NULL) && (--m != 0));
```

2. 6   Reading Files

With the internal representation in place, we can now easily read in the input file by supplying an appropriate file pointer to function readFile().

```
#define MAXBUF 72

void readFile(FILE *fp)
{
    char buf[MAXBUF];

    while (fgets(buf, MAXBUF, fp) != NULL) {
        char *c;
        if (buf[strlen(buf)-1] == '\n')
            buf[strlen(buf)-1] = '\0';
        c = malloc(strlen(buf)+1); strcpy(c, buf);
        append(c);
    }
}
```

The function readFile() relies on fgets() to read each line from the file as represented by the file pointer fp. A NULL return result implies the end-of-file condition, and thus terminates the loop. Note that there are two blocks in the function, both of them with local variable definitions.

The #define preprocessor directive defines a macro so that occurrences of MAXBUF in the source file is replaced by 72. Macro substitution is often used because C does not provide a constant definition construct.

The fgets() library routine requires three parameters when reading in a string of characters:

- the address of the buffer to hold what is to be read

- the size of that buffer, and

- the file pointer which represents the file to read from

The size of the buffer is significant because it prevents fgets() from reading more characters than the buffer can hold. Using memory areas beyond what has been allocated exposes the very likely possibility that such areas are used for two purposes. Interference of this kind leads to inconsistency and possibly intermittent program errors. Thus, fgets() reads and returns the string up till a newline character, or up to one less than the size of the buffer (since string representation in C requires a zero-value byte terminator, as elaborated below).

The construct char buf[MAXBUF] defines an array with MAXBUF elements. Since array subscripts start from 0, the last element is buf[MAXBUF-1]. Arrays in C are peculiar in one other aspect: while buf[2] returns the third element, buf on its own returns the address of the array (and not the array contents, as one would expect from Pascal). This address is thus supplied to fgets().

Due to the varied lengths of strings, C treats strings as *character sequences* terminated by the ASCII null (\0) character[1]. strlen(buf) returns the length of the string stored at the address associated with buf. Note that string length need not be the array size of buf, and as such, strlen() is applied to it. strlen() returns the length of a string by counting the number of characters until the first null character. Since array subscripts in C start from 0, buf[strlen(buf)-1] returns the last character read.

If this is a newline character ('\n'), it is discarded because that is already implied by our representation. When it is not a newline character, the long line is implicitly divided into shorter fragments. In this case, remaining characters are read into a subsequent Line structure. This partitioning ensures that each line can be easily displayed in the available screen width[2].

The array buf is merely a local buffer used by fgets() to read a display line during each iteration of the loop. Therefore, a new memory block must be allocated afresh for each line. Each allocation makes a request to malloc() for a memory block of size one more than the length of the line (because of the zero-value byte terminator).

As malloc() returns the base address of the block of n characters requested, it is assigned to character pointer c. The use of dynamic arrays[3], as in this case, is subtle: since c addresses a memory block, it may also be viewed as the address of the first array element. The address given by an array name is merely the situation in reverse. The next address location is equivalent to the second element and so on. In this way, such blocks may be treated as arrays with elements *c, *(c+1), *(c+2), etc.

The line contents in buf are copied to a new region via strcpy(). Note the difference between the three statements:

```
c = buf;
*c = *buf;
memcpy(c, buf, N);
```

---

[1] Note that the null character and the NULL pointer have the same value of 0 but they are not for any arithmetic operations. The former is the ASCII character zero, and the latter indicates the absence of a valid object.

[2] This simplification is not totally sound because such truncated lines cannot be distinguished from shorter lines. Nevertheless, it suffices for a simplistic toy demonstration program.

[3] Dynamic arrays are those whose sizes are only determined at run time.

Since an array name in C returns the address of its first element, the first statement assigns the address of buffer buf to character pointer c. The second statement involves indirect reference of character pointers, and so only the first character of the line is copied. The third statement copies the contents of the N-sized block, referenced by buf, to that referenced by c. This is the semantics of the strcpy() function, N-1 being the length of the string.

2. 7   Interpreting User Requests

Following start-up initialisation, the browser merely needs to read and interpret the user's navigation requests. The processing loop repeatedly involves

- providing feedback via display of current context,

- reading a user command, and

- adjusting the new focus appropriately according to user request.

Feedback of the current context is provided by the function display() seen earlier. A single-character user command may be read using the library routine getchar().

```
#define LINES 24

void readCommandsAndInterpret()
{
  int more = 1;

  while (more) {
    char c;

    display(LINES-1);
    printf("n)ext page p)revious page q)uit");
    c = getchar();
    printf("\n");
    switch (c) {
      case ' ':
      case 'n':
        forward(LINES-2);
        break;
      case 'p':
        backward(LINES-2);
        break;
      case 'q':
        more = 0;
        break;
    }
  }
}
```

Based on the command character, control is dispatched to the appropriate code fragment via a switch construct. It provides a multi-way selection facility and is similar to the Pascal case statement, except that a break statement must be explicitly placed, to terminate execution of the case limb. In the absence of an explicit branch instruction, execution proceeds to the next limb, just as the case for limbs ' ' and 'n'. A switch statement without a matching case limb has no effect.

In the simplest case, commands must allow the user to scroll forward and backward a screenful at a time. Currently, the simplistic approach assumes a 24-line terminal display. With one line reserved for prompting, each scroll forward or backward is two less than this maximum so that one other line of context information is always visible across the page.

Since boolean variables are not provided in C, the integer variable more is used to signal termination when 'q' is pressed. Alternatively, since no computation is required following the switch or the while statement, a return statement might also be used to exit from the function readCommandsAndInterpret().

2. 8   Initialising the Browser

What remains to be done in the main program is appropriate initialisation: to obtain the name of the file to be browsed, and ensure that it actually exists.

The function main() is special because in C it is the first function to be invoked. The *stdio* library function gets() reads a string denoting the name of the file to be browsed. As with fgets() which we encountered previously, gets(name) reads a string into the location associated with the character array name.

```
main()
{
    char name[100];
    FILE *fd;

    printf("file: ");
    gets(name);
    fd = fopen(name, "r");
    if (fd == NULL) {
        printf("cannot open %s\n", name);
        exit(1);
    }
    readFile(fd);
    fclose(fd);
    home();
    readCommandsAndInterpret();
}
```

The library call `fopen()` opens the file for reading (as specified by the second parameter `"r"`). It returns a corresponding file pointer so that subsequent operations are made through it. Such library calls provide some degree of information hiding in that I/O operations may be performed without knowing of the contents of each `FILE` data structure. This file pointer is passed to `readFile` so that the contents of the file may be read into the internal representation as described earlier.

2. 9   Improvements to the Browser

The browser implementation meets its required objective, but is nevertheless crude. Subsequent chapters will consider how the implementation can be improved.

The display mechanism should be the first to undergo improvement. It completely reprints a view regardless of current screen contents. An better display would only print portions of the screen that are different over two consecutive views. This would be beneficial when scrolling one line forward or backward.

Addressing portions of the screen for selective update is typically terminal dependent. A strategy for use with various types of display hardware is required.

Reading user commands interactively in the default line mode is currently clumsy because a newline character is required before the contents of a line can be read. Reading keystrokes immediately would be more convenient for users.

The UNIX system is flexible in its treatment of files and devices. UNIX programs often do not distinguish between reading from a file, a keyboard, or for that matter, the output of another program. It would thus be useful to provide the flexibility of browsing through the output of another program. This is straightforward for a batched program operating on the output of another program through a pipe into its standard input stream. However, interactive applications are constrained in that user commands are also expected from the standard input stream. This implies that standard input contents must be distinguished from command keystrokes. Program parameters too should be specified at the command line.

2. 10   Summary

This chapter has provided a glimpse of the C programming language via a simple browser program for displaying files. The following language features were covered:

§   variable definition

```
int a, b;
```

§   record definition and instances

```
struct rt {
  int a, b;
} r;

r.b = r.a;
```

§   array definition and instances

```
struct rt s[100];

s[a] = s[b];
```

§   function definition and parameters

```
int max(int a, b)
{
   ...
}
```

§   assignment and arithmetic operators, and function calls

§   while, do, if-else and switch control-flow constructs

§   input and output using FILE pointers, fgets(), gets(), getchar() and printf()

§   dynamic memory allocation using malloc()

§   string operations via strlen() and strcpy()

The browser implementation will be gradually refined when more C and UNIX facilities are studied in subsequent chapters.

2. 11   Exercises

1. The code for the browser may be found in browser.c. Note that it is the same as that described in this chapter. Copy it into your directory area and compile it by reading ahead to the next chapter to see how it might be done.

2. Run the browser to view the original source code using the command:

```
$ a.out
file: browser.c
```

3. a.out is the default name given to executable files generated by most UNIX compilers. Rename the recently produced executable program to something more appropriate.

4. Edit the function `readCommandsAndInterpret` so that it interprets your favourite key bindings for the scrolling commands. Provide a more suitable user prompt if necessary.

5. Make your own list of the browser's shortcomings as well as your wish list of desirable features.

3

The Run-time Organisation of C Programs

Programming in a high-level language implies a degree of insulation from machine details and language implementation issues. However, some understanding of the implementation of C and run-time considerations is beneficial and important for proficient use of the language. As mentioned earlier, C is not a restrictive language. It is permissive in that it allows the programmer a greater deal of freedom in manipulating program entities.

Some background knowledge of the run-time organisation of C programs therefore provides a better understanding of C constructs, desirable programming styles, and pitfalls to be avoided.

3.1 Program Compilation

A C program is prepared as an ASCII text file. It is thus not directly executable on typical machine hardware. Machine execution requires that appropriate machine code be loaded into the memory of the host machine. The first task of the C compiler is to analyse C programs. Where it does not discover any specification errors, it generates suitable machine code to implement the equivalent program semantics. This implies that the semantics of the particular program is known and not ambiguous.

Assuming that the C compiler used is gcc[1], the browser program in the file browser.c may be compiled via:

```
$ gcc browser.c
```

---

[1] gcc is the GNU C compiler distributed by the Free Software Foundation.

If the compilation is successful, the executable code is written out to the default output file, namely, a.out. To prevent it from being overwritten by the next compilation, it may be renamed to browser by using the standard UNIX command mv. Alternatively, the -o option in gcc may be used to specify the name of the output file:

```
$ gcc -o browser browser.c
```

3. 2   Run-time Organisation of a Program

When a program is selected for execution, its compiled codes are loaded into an appropriate memory block in the host machine. The address space for a program is typically organised into three segments: a code segment, a data segment and a stack segment. This is illustrated in Figure 3-1.

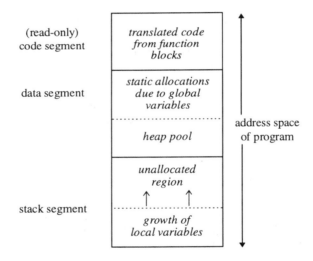

Figure 3-1: Run-time memory organisation

Since the executable code of a C program is not modified after compilation, the code segment is typically marked as read-only. This ensures that the code segment can be shared with another invocation of the same program. The data and stack segments however cannot be shared. Each invocation must have its own data and stack segments so that the processes do not interact with each other non-deterministically.

Global variables, such as a and b, are allocated memory in the data segment as and when their definitions are encountered by the compiler.

```
int a;

void f()
{
   ...
}

int b;
```

In this case, variables might be allocated adjacent memory areas even if they were separated in the original source by function f().

A global variable may be initialised with a value. The data region associated with global variables may then be accordingly sub-divided into initialised and uninitialised sections. Initialised data is set up at compile time. Thus, an exact image is merely loaded at the start of program execution. This static nature of initialisation arises because variables may only be initialised from constant expressions and not from variables or the result of function calls. Uninitialised data need not be represented by the loader, except for the size of the uninitialised data block required.

Local variables, such as c and d, which are declared in function bodies are however not allocated memory in the data segment.

```
void g()
{
   int c, d;

   ...
   if ...
      g();
}
```

An important consideration here is the possibility of recursive calls. Each recursive function call requires the storage allocation for an independent set of local variables. Storage for local variables are thus said to be dynamically allocated when the function is invoked, and similarly, deallocated when control returns to the caller.

While initialisations of local variables are permitted, these are performed on function entry, and thus differ from the case of global variables. They merely serve as syntactic facilities instead of introducing a new feature. The two fragments in Figure 3-2 are equivalent.

```
void g()                              void g()
{                                     {
    int. *c = pointer_value,              int *c, d;
        d = int_value;
                                          c = pointer_value;
                                          d = int_value;
    . . .                                 . . .
}                                     }
```

Figure 3-2: Initialisation of local variables

With nested function calls, the first function to be invoked will be the last to exit. Similarly, storage for the local variables declared in the first function to be invoked is allocated first and deallocated last. It is appropriate to allocate local variables separately from global variables since the existence of the former is closely related to the function call-graph and follows last-in-first-out (LIFO) order. The stack segment is thus used for such storage allocation in LIFO order.

A function call also requires storage for preserving the system information of the caller so that it can be restored on returning from a function call. Probably the most significant of this information is the caller's return address which allows control to return at the end of a function. Machine registers which are used across a function call must also be preserved accordingly.

Most language implementations combine the tasks of allocating storage for local variables with those for system information. The storage requirements of the former tend to vary with declarations, while that of the latter tend to be constant. Such a memory block to maintain the state of a function activation is typically known as an *activation record*. The stack segment would contain a list of activation records; each record representing an active function (i.e. invoked but not yet terminated).

3. 3   Allocation of Heap Storage

There are also situations where storage allocation and deallocation do not follow the LIFO ordering exhibited by local variables. Instead of being predetermined by the structure of the program, allocations and deallocations of heap variables are explicitly controlled by the programmer. This is evident with a list data structure where items are added at one end (as in a queue situation), but removed selectively.

The file representation of the browser in chapter 2 illustrates another situation where storage allocation is not related to program structure. In that situation, storage is explicitly allocated in functions append() and readfile(), but kept for the lifetime of the program.

In such cases, we use heap allocations via function calls like `malloc()` and `free()`. `malloc(n)` is a general heap allocator which returns the location where a block of n bytes has been reserved. It ensures that the location will not be reallocated so that its integrity is ensured. `free(p)` is the complementary function which returns the memory block addressed by p back to the heap pool so that it can be reallocated by `malloc()`.

The heap manager library routines allocate heap memory from space left over in the data segment after global variable requirements are satisfied. Appropriate system structures must be maintained to track allocated and allocable regions. In UNIX, `malloc()` may request, via the `sbrk()` system call, to extend the data segment in order to obtain more heap space.

3. 4   Pointer Indirection

A heap variable differs from a global or local variable in that it does not have an explicit name by which it will be referenced. Instead, a heap variable is referenced by its address. The function `malloc()` returns the address of the allocated heap block. Henceforth, access of the variable is by using this address. Therefore, the address of a heap variable, as returned by `malloc()`, is always assigned to an appropriate pointer variable. A heap variable is referenced *through* the pointer variable by the use of indirection operator "*". (The term "indirection" implies that there is an additional reference to access the heap variable.)

```
void f()
{
    int i;
    int *pi;

    i = 5;
    pi = malloc(sizeof(int));
    if (pi != NULL)
        *pi = 100;
}
```

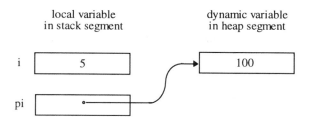

Figure 3-3: Side-effect of function f()

Note that a heap variable will not be accessible when references to it no longer exist. When function f() terminates, the storage areas for local variables i and pi are reclaimed. If the heap reference contained in pi is not assigned elsewhere, it will be lost. A heap variable in this situation is referred to as a *dangling object* because while it still exists, it is useless because it cannot be referenced. Dangling objects should be avoided because they are not reclaimed by most heap managers and continue to take up memory resources.

C is more permissive than Pascal in that the address-of operator "&" returns the address of any variable. This address may in turn be assigned to an appropriate pointer variable, just as in the case with malloc() allocations. Pointer indirection provides an additional means of accessing local variables.

```
void g()
{
    int i;
    int *pi;
    int **ppi;

    i = 5;

    pi = &i;      *pi = 5;

    ppi = &pi;   **ppi = 5;
}
```

In the code fragment above, the value 5 may be directly assigned to i, but indirectly assigned via pi or ppi. The situation is graphically represented below. In this case, an indirection operator could be equated to "following an arrow" to a new location.

Figure 3-4: Pointer indirection

3. 5   Legitimate Memory Access

It is important that only pointers with legitimate (address) values be indirectly referenced. In this respect, the predefined value of NULL does not signify a legitimate address, and should not be used for pointer indirection.

The `malloc()` routine uses this convention. It returns the value NULL when there is insufficient heap memory. Since there is the possibility that the memory allocation request cannot be granted, programs must check for this condition.

However, apart from the value NULL, it is often not possible to tell if a pointer value describes the legitimate location of a variable. A prudent programmer must ensure that a pointer should be

- NULL,

- the address of a global variable,

- the address of a local variable of an active function, or

- the address of an allocated heap location.

Note that a legitimate pointer reference might become illegitimate if the corresponding location is subsequently deallocated. For the case of a reference to a local variable, it should not continue after the function has exited, since the set of local variables would have been deallocated. This situation is demonstrated via the code fragment below and corresponding graphical representations in Figure 3-5 and Figure 3-6:

```
int *p;

void m()
{
    int k;

    ...
    p = &k;
}

void n()
{
    m();
    /* p now references an unallocated memory region */
}
```

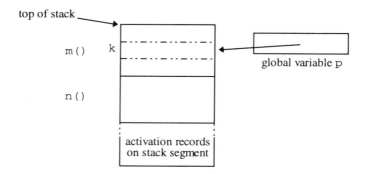

Figure 3-5: Stack contents when m() *is active*

If no other functions are called after m() terminates, the location above the stack top might remain unallocated, and further (illegitimate) pointer references to that location would seem to be correct.

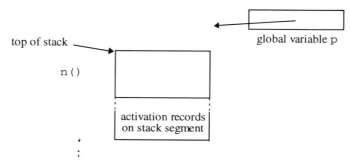

Figure 3-6: Stack contents when m() *has terminated and* n() *is active*

However, with subsequent function calls, the location at the stack top is reallocated to local variables. The result is an unexpected overwriting of memory values, and this is when erroneous symptoms show.

A similar situation occurs with dangling pointer references, as seen with the following sample fragment. When the location reference by p is reclaimed via the call to free(p), q will still reference the same location. However, it is no longer a legitimately allocated location.

```
void bad()
{
   int *p; int *q;

   p = malloc(sizeof(int));
   if (p == NULL) error("no heap memory");
   q = p;
   ...
   free(p);
   ...
   *q = 20;
}
```

If the heap deallocator free() does not write onto the deallocated variable, continued access of the location via *q might not seem erroneous. However, if the location is subsequently reallocated, unexpected overwriting, as in the previous case, occurs.

A more damaging situation can occur. If the deallocated location becomes part of the system data structure for maintaining the heap pool, inconsistent information might be captured due to overwriting from the program's incorrect code. This can cause unpredictable behaviour in the heap management routines themselves!

To summarise, manipulating an unallocated location in memory must always be avoided due to the unpredictable consequences. In this respect, dereferencing any stray pointer value is erroneous, even if the ill-effects are not immediately evident. If by coincidence, an illegitimate pointer references an unused location, the effect might not be significant immediately. However, undesirable interactions will occur when that location is ultimately used. On the other hand, if an illegitimate pointer references an existing variable location, the effects of such aliasing would be unexpected overwriting of variable values.

3. 6   Modular Structure

Useful C programs are typically large, and hence some form of modularisation is very helpful for both readability, writability and efficient recompilation. Since C does not provide a module construct, it is popular practice to rely on files as units of compilation. It is helpful then that modifications to, for instance, two files out of a total of ten to form a program would require between two to ten recompilations (due to possible interactions which make recompilation of unchanged units necessary). However, even for the most minor modifications, a large program in a file will always require a vast compilation effort.

Because human intellect is limited, subdividing a program allows us to better focus our thoughts on less complex concerns. It is also good practice to modularise a program logically such that related code and data definitions appear together in the same unit. This is consistent with abstraction techniques and makes code reusability possible.

For example, it is likely that a program to evaluate postfix expressions requires the use of an integer stack. In this case, it is useful that the development of the stack module and the expression evaluator proper proceed separately. A good starting point is to realise the interface between the two program units.

A stack data type might include primitive operations to:

- push an integer on the stack,

- inquire what the size of the stack is, and

- pop the top integer from the stack.

This could translate to the following C declarations:

```
void push(int);
int size();
int pop();
```

By using such declarations, an expression evaluator could be implemented in a file to be named eval.c, as shown in Listing 3-1.

```
void push(int);
int size();
int pop();

int ch;

int getnumber()
{
  int n = 0;
  while (ch>='0' && ch <='9') {
     n = n*10 + ch-'0';
     ch = getchar();
  }
  return(n);
}

main()
{
  ch = getchar();
  while (ch != EOF) {
    switch (ch) {
      case '0': case '1': case '2': case '3': case '4':
      case '5': case '6': case '7': case '8': case '9':
        push(getnumber());
        break;
      case '+':
        if (size() < 2) {
            printf("to few arguments\n");
```

```
            exit(1);
        } else
            push(pop() + pop());
        ch = getchar();
        break;
    case ' ':
        ch = getchar();
        break;
    }
  }
}
```

Listing 3-1: Expression evaluator

Similarly, the stack implementation may proceed independently in another file to be named `stack.c`. This is illustrated in Listing 3-2.

```
int stack[100];
int top = 0;

void push(int x)
{
    stack[top++] = x;
}

int size()
{
    return(top);
}

int pop()
{
    return(stack[--top]);
}
```

Listing 3-2: Implementation of stack functionality

In the case of separate program files, the C compiler must also analyse each file independently. It can only produce object code with placeholders for external labels. When compiling `eval.c` to produce the object file `eval.o`, the references to `push`, `size` and `pop` are unknown since the exact locations of these non-local entities are defined elsewhere in `stack.c`. On the other hand, when `stack.c` is compiled, the corresponding object file `stack.o` would "advertise" that it has the addresses for public labels `push`, `size` and `pop`. These situations are illustrated in Figure 3-7.

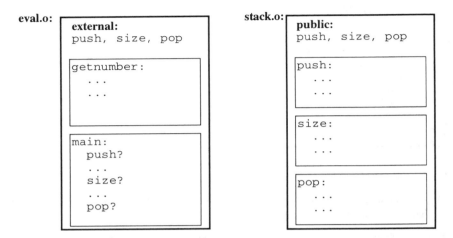

Figure 3-7: Object module representation

It is the linker's task to match external labels with public labels. The result is a concatenation of object files, with placeholders replaced by addresses of appropriate labels:

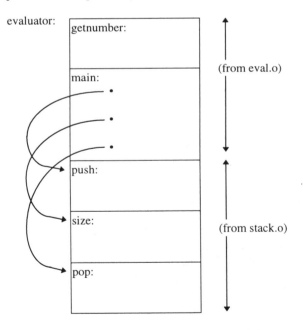

Figure 3-8: Result of linking object modules

Lastly, modular structure requires some insight into the compilation procedure. UNIX compilers usually combine the task of compiling with linking. Thus, when browser.c was compiled via gcc browser.c, a corresponding object file browser.o was first produced, followed by the linker stage to produce the executable file a.out. Language details of external and public declarations are further discussed in chapter 5.

To compile separate files, such as stack.c and eval.c, the "-c" option must be specified. This prevents the linker from being invoked until all object files are available:

```
$ gcc -c eval.c
$ gcc -c stack.c
```

Subsequently, the linker is invoked to link the resultant object files. If all external symbols can be resolved, the linker produces an executable file:

```
$ gcc eval.o stack.o
```

For argument's sake, if eval.c was compiled without the "-c" flag, the linker (invoked by default) would complain that the symbols push, size and pop have not been defined. If stack.c was similarly compiled, the linker would complain that main() has not been defined. This is due to the convention that main() is the first C function to be invoked, and thus is always expected by the C run-time library.

3. 7 Libraries

A program may comprise a number of source files depending on task decomposition. In this case, linking a large number of object files might prove to be tedious. Often, a group of object files might be "pre-gathered" so that it may be used across a suite of applications. Such a group of object files is known as a library.

A library that is almost always used when producing executables is the standard C library. It contains frequently used routines for performing useful tasks which might not be defined in the C language. One such task is program initialisation. Among other things, program initialisation requires that memory segments be set up appropriately, and program arguments be accessible. In addition, program finalisation code is required to close files which have been left opened.

The standard C library implements initialisation and finalisation tasks through a routine call _main(). It then makes a call to main() when initialisation is completed. This is why all C programs must define the special function main(). The library also includes a set of interface functions through which operating-system kernel calls are made.

Some operating system kernel calls are discussed in Part II. User-defined libraries will be further discussed in chapter 4.

3. 8   Preprocessor Directives

We have seen that preprocessor directives are indicated by a "#" symbol in the first column of a C source program. The commonly used directives allow for

- file inclusion #include,

- macro definition via #define, and

- conditional directives #if, #ifdef, #else and #endif.

a. File inclusion

File inclusion allows another file to be included in the compilation in place of the directive. This facility is useful for including common-interface information into more than one file. In the expression-evaluator example, the interface information consisted of only three lines, and was only required by eval.c. The situation is not always as convenient.

It is not uncommon for interface information to exceed 50 lines of C declarations, and be required in more than one file. Duplicating code over these files is tedious, and maintaining consistency across all files is also problematic.

Interface information is better kept in a separate file, say, stack.h. This file may then be included into eval.c via a #include preprocessor directive. It is even recommended that it be included into stack.c to ensure that interfaces are in fact consistent with the declarations there. In general, it must be included into every source file that requires such interface information.

If double quotes ("   ") are used to delimit the file name, the preprocessor searches for it in the current directory. If angle brackets (<   >) are used, the file is included from predefined system directories. This is the situation for system-defined interface files.

b. Macro substitution

We have also seen the #define macro definition facility which specifies textual substitution. The macro definition example below replaces all subsequent occurrences of LINES with 24 during macro processing:

```
#define LINES 24
```

Parameters are also allowed such that formal parameters are substituted with actual arguments when the body of a definition is expanded. The macro definition example below replaces all occurrences of max(x, y) with the macro body:

```
#define max(a,b) (a>b?a:b)
```

However, within the body, a and b are replaced with appropriate arguments – in this case, x and y, whatever x and y may be.

c. Conditional compilation

A conditional directive allows different fragments of code to be compiled depending on a specific compile-time condition. It is thus similar to the if-else conditional statement in that it allows various fragments of code to be executed depending on a condition. The significant difference is that the decision to include code fragments to be compiled (and thus included into the object file) is made at compile time and not run time.

The various conditional compilation directives are summarised in Table 3-1.

Form	Example instance	Remarks

`#ifdef sym`
`    code`
`#endif`
`#ifndef sym`
`    code`
`#endif`
`#ifdef sym`
`    code`
`#else`
`    code`
`#endif`
	`#ifdef DEBUG`
	`    assert(p != NULL, "p = NULL");`
	`#endif`
	`#ifndef DEBUG`
	`    performFullQuery();`
	`#endif`
		Include the code fragment for compilation if the symbol DEBUG is defined. Include the code fragment for compilation if the symbol DEBUG is not defined.

`#if (expn)`
`    code`
`#endif`
`#if (expn)`
`    code1`
`#else`
`    code2`
`#endif`
	`#if (SYSV || BSD)`
	`    printf("UNIX");`
	`#endif`
	`#if (UNIX)`
	`    printf("UNIX");`
	`#else`
	`    printf("OTHERS");`
	`#endif`
		Include the code fragment for compilation if expn evaluates to non zero. Include code1 fragment for compilation if expn evaluates to non zero, else include code2 fragment for compilation.

Table 3-1: Preprocessor directives

As suggested by the examples above, this conditional compilation facility may be used as an assert() debugging aid, as well as for configuration control. Instead of inserting and deleting (or hiding them within comments), the DEBUG symbol may be used to control the inclusion of run-time assertion. In this instance, the assert macro might be defined as:

```
#ifdef DEBUG
#define assert(c,m) if (!(c)) {                \
                        printf("%s\n", m);  \
                        exit(1);            \
                    }
#endif
```

Note that where a macro definition extends beyond a line, a backslash "\" is used as a continuation marker. This is standard UNIX practice where an "escape" sequence signifies that the next character should be used literally instead. In this case, it is a newline character, rather than its special semantics indicating the end of a macro definition.

As for configuration control, platform or hardware specific code may be specified and isolated by delimiting them within conditional compilation directives. The symbols involved in conditional compilation expressions are those defined using the same #define directive. Compiling with the DEBUG and BSD modes would then only involve putting the following lines before all others which refer to them:

```
#define DEBUG
#define BSD   1
#define SYSV  0
```

d. Preprocessor implementation

The implementation of the compiler proper is broken down into various subtasks and connected via pipes[2] or by using temporary files. The preprocessor is typically a separate program invoked as part of the compiler task of program analysis. This is very much consistent with the UNIX philosophy of program reusability and combining the functionality of smaller and simpler programs. This framework is graphically illustrated in Figure 3-9.

---

[2] Pipes are elaborated in chapter 8.

compiler:

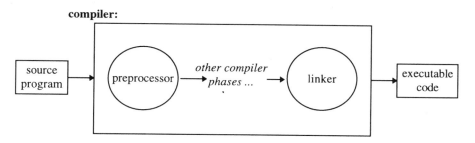

Figure 3-9: Organisation of C compiler

Program source lines beginning with "#" signal a preprocessor statement and are processed accordingly. All other lines without directives pass through the preprocessor, possibly with appropriate macro substitution.

3. 9 Function **main()** and Program Parameters

As mentioned earlier, the function main() is special in that it is the first function to be invoked. The standard C library has therefore arranged it so that it is called with the appropriate program arguments in a standard format. This format consists of the count of arguments argc and an array argv (of the same size) of character strings. The echo program in Listing 3-3 prints out all program arguments.

```
/* print program arguments */
main (int argc, char *argv[])
{
    int i;

    for (i = 0; i<argc; i++)
        printf("%s\n", argv[i]);
}
```

Listing 3-3: Program to print out command line arguments

The echo program shows two instances where the number of array elements cannot be determined until run time: the number of program arguments and the length of each argument are both unknown until the program is invoked.

C solves this dynamic-array situation by not concerning itself with the number of array elements, but with the base address of the array and the type of elements instead. Remember that an array is merely represented by the address of its first element. Since array elements are held in a contiguous block of memory, subsequent array elements are at fixed offsets from the first element. These offsets would be determined by the size of intervening array elements. This is in turn determined by the element type.

A string in C is essentially a character sequence. It is represented by the address of its first character byte. As an added convention, the compiler and string-manipulation routines always add a zero-value byte null terminator (\0).

Each program argument can thus be represented as a character pointer char *. It references some memory which has been appropriately allocated. An array of such strings would thus have been a consecutive block of pointers to individual character arrays, thus char *[][3]. This is graphically illustrated in Figure 3-10.

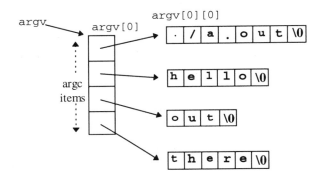

Figure 3-10: Argument list for $ ./a.out hello out there

Since argv is an address of a string (i.e., address of a character), argv[0] addresses the first string, and argv[0][0] returns the first character of that string. By convention, the first parameter argv[0] is the program name.

3.10   Summary

The following points were discussed in this chapter:

§   Compilation involves understanding the semantics of a program and then generating appropriate equivalent machine code to facilitate execution.

§   A C program comprises of code, data and stack segments at run time. Global variables are allocated space in the data segment, and local variables are allocated space in the stack segment.

---

[3]   Such declarators are elaborated on in chapter 5.

§   Heap space allows for flexible memory request and deallocation. To prevent overwriting of values, only allocated memory blocks should be used.

§   Programs should be decomposed based on functionality. C allows for modules via independent compilation and linkage.

§   The use of libraries and the preprocessor help in a productive programming style.

3. 11   Exercises

1.   Copy the files `eval.c` and `stack.c` into your own directory area. Make an attempt to compile and link both files. Do not execute them as the main processing loop in `eval.c` does not yet have facilities to print out the results of an evaluation.

   Add code to `eval.c` to implement additional arithmetic operators and printing facilities.

2.   Find out what happens when global definitions with the same name appear in different program files. Similarly, see what happens when a definition is not found in any program file.

3.   Modularise the browser program appropriately. Code fragments for representing a file, displaying the file contents and navigating to various portions of a file might be placed in separate program modules.

4.   Instead of reading the name of the file to be browsed, allow it to be specified in the command line.

4

Using *curses* for Interactive Applications

The file browser in chapter 2 is a simple implementation to illustrate some of the facilities available in C. It is significantly lacking in terms of its display strategy. Improvements are possible by using the features found in modern terminals. Such features might include cursor addressing and hardware-supported scrolling. Instead of redrawing the whole screen area to display a new context, it is often more efficient if only modified portions of the screen are redrawn.

In this chapter, we will see how libraries might code reusability, and how interactive display and keyboard input are simplified by using the *termcap* and *curses* libraries.

4. 1 Objectives of *termcap* and *curses* Libraries

The proposed improvements to the browser display highlight the potential problem of terminal-device dependency. By using the custom features of a terminal, the browser is henceforth restricted to run only with that particular terminal.

Most modern terminals allow for direct cursor addressing, a variety of screen attributes, character/line insertion and deletion. Table 4-1 shows sample special character sequences for the VT100 and Health 19 terminals. Sending these sequences to the respective terminals would achieve the corresponding effects:

Functionality	VT102 sequence	Health 19 sequence	Remarks
cursor addressing	ESC [*m* ; *n* H	ESC Y *j* *k*	*m* and *n* are numeric strings and *j* and *k* are ASCII codes which denote destination screen coordinates
screen attributes	ESC [7 m ESC [0 m	ESC p ESC q	turn reverse video on turn reverse video off

Table 4-1: Sample terminal control sequences

The *termcap* library offers the flexibility of using the custom features of a particular terminal, but without hardwiring those characteristics into the application code. It maintains a list of popular terminal models with corresponding capabilities. This might include how to move the cursor, insert and delete characters, insert and delete lines, and change display attributes. An appropriate format is chosen for the *termcap* database file, together with suitable library routines to extract specifications.

A program which uses the *termcap* library will first check the "TERM" environment variable[1] for an indication of the terminal brand used. This information may be set by the local system administrators, by terminal identification sequences to identify terminal models, or in the user's .profile. With the terminal brand known, the *termcap* initialisation routine may proceed with initialisation routines to obtain the corresponding set of terminal control sequences. These will then be used to manipulate the display.

The *termcap* library allows custom terminal features to be used without restricting the application to the use of a specific terminal model. However, the other issue of obtaining efficient screen updates is solved by the *curses* library. Briefly, the *curses* library maintains two screen maps: one of the existing display, and the other of the intended display. It also has appropriate logic to compare the two maps to determine which portions of the physical screen require updating. However, the ultimate task of writing to the screen is still dependent on the *termcap* library.

It is noteworthy that these issues of screen handling do not pertain only to the browser application. In general, they apply to all interactive programs which require selective screen updates and cursor addressing. Thus, packaging these functionalities into libraries allow for convenient reuse. Software reusability not only reduces software development costs, it also provides a consistent model for both users and programmers.

---

[1] Environment variables are further discussed in chapter 8.

4. 2   A Basic I/O Interface for Interactive Applications

The *curses* library provides a minimal but sufficient interface for typical interactive applications. Hence, the strategy works with most terminals. In fact, the *curses* library was implemented during the period when standard terminals had limited functionality. Recent variants of the *curses* library from different vendors provide some improvement.

In any case, the updating routines attempt to make the most of the terminal characteristics. For example, if the terminal is specified as possessing hardware-scrolling capabilities, using the feature when scrolling increases the effectiveness of screen updates. If that feature is not present, *curses* will redraw the affected screen region.

The basic *curses* functionality is reviewed in this section to enable some improvements to be made to the browser implementation. It allows an application to:

- reposition the cursor (and thus, also set a new insertion location),
- write to the screen,
- set screen attributes, and
- read from the keyboard in non-canonical mode[2].

a. Initialisation and finalisation

The function prototypes of *curses* routines are found in `curses.h` and they are included into a program via the preprocessor include directive:

```
#include <curses.h>
```

The *curses* function `initscr()` initialises data structures which will be used by other *curses* routines. It must be invoked at the start of the program before any other *curses* functions. The function `endwin()` is the complementary routine. It deallocates appropriate data structures when the *curses* functionality is no longer required. It also resets the terminal to the original settings.

```
void initscr();
void endwin();
```

---

[2] Canonical mode is the name given to reading the keyboard on a line-by-line basis. Here, input is only available following a newline character. In non-canonical mode, input is available regardless of whether a newline character is encountered.

b. Screen output

The functions `addch()` and `addstr()` output a character and character string respectively at the current cursor position:

```
void addch(char);
void addstr(char *);
```

The function `printw()` allows for formatted output. It is the *curses* equivalent of the `printf()` function that we saw earlier in chapter 2.

```
void printw(char *, ...);
```

c. Cursor positioning

The cursor may be positioned via the function `move()`. The x and y coordinates are supplied as arguments. The origin (0,0) denotes the top left corner of the screen.

```
void move(int y, int x);
```

d. Screen attributes

Screen bold attributes may be turned on and off via the functions `standout()` and `standend()` respectively:

```
void standout();
void standend();
```

e. Selective screen erase

The entire screen may be cleared via the function `erase()`. This is equivalent to writing spaces to every position in the screen.

```
void erase();
```

Selective deletion within a line is performed by the function `clrtoeol()`. It clears from the current cursor position to the end of the line. The related function `clrtobot()` clears to the bottom of the screen.

```
void clrtoeol();
void clrtobot();
```

f. Screen refresh

Screen updates cannot be optimized unless the side-effects of the manipulation functions described earlier are delayed. The *curses* library works by delaying physical screen updates for as long as possible, until it reaches a stage specified by the programmer when a view must be displayed on the terminal screen. The function `refresh()` essentially performs this task.

```
void refresh();
```

It compares the (new) intended view with that which currently exists (as constructed for the previous `refresh()` operation) and performs appropriate write operations onto the terminal screen to maintain view consistency, as illustrated in Figure 4-1.

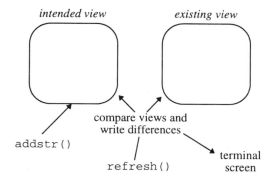

Figure 4-1: View consistency

This delay-and-compare strategy allows for two kinds of optimisation. Firstly, comparison of two views allows modified portions of the screen to be identified. Thus, rewriting only modified portions reduces output traffic. Note that comparisons in a piecemeal fashion cannot be as effective as comparing a total view. Even if screen updates are necessary, knowledge of the complete screen display allows it to be written with minimal cursor movements. Secondly, bulk output in this case, as compared to character-by-character writes, may be handled by device drivers, and reduces the overheads of kernel operations.

g. Keyboard input

Interactive programs not only write to the screen, but also require input from the keyboard. *curses* provide facilities to handle the keyboard and UNIX terminal modes. The keyboard may be read via the function getch():

```
int getch();
```

This function will also recognise function and numeric pad keys which emit extended codes. These will be further discussed in subsequent sections.

The exact behaviour of function getch() is altered depending on the input mode. Reading in canonical or non-canonical modes may be specified by nocbreak() and cbreak() respectively:

```
void nocbreak();
void cbreak();
```

Similarly, reading with system echoing is enabled or disabled by echo() and noecho() respectively:

```
void echo();
void noecho();
```

These modes are used in varied circumstances. Reading in non-canonical mode without echoing might be useful when reading single-character commands and acting on them immediately. This situation typically occurs when using text editors such as vi.

Reading in canonical mode implies that keyboard codes are stored in the buffer of the device driver and are not available until a newline key. This is useful when reading a string of characters. In this instance, the echo mode is typically enabled.

Note that *curses* does not actually implement the necessary buffering operations or input echoing. Instead, *curses* makes appropriate system calls to the terminal device driver. In general, the terminal device driver has other functionalities. These are discussed in chapter 11.

4. 3   Improving the File Browser

Changes to the browser code will now be described. The full listing is reproduced in browser1.c.

a. Interface file

Since input and output is now performed using the *curses* library, the interface file "curses.h" is included instead. Since "stdio.h" is included within "curses.h", it need not be included by the browser.

```
#include <curses.h>
```

b. Displaying a page

While the logic in function display() remains the same, it now uses the functions erase(), move() and printw(). It prepares a clean screen, moves to the appropriate screen location and outputs the line contents appropriately.

```
void display(int m)
{
  struct Line *display = current;
  int lineNum = lineNumber;
  int i = 0;

  erase();
  do {
    move(i++, 0);
    printw("%4d   %s", lineNum++, display->contents);
    display = display->next;
    m--;
  } while ((display != NULL) && (m != 0));
}
```

The variable i maintains the row number of the line currently being displayed, and is initialised to 0 since the coordinate starts from zero.

The function move() allows the destination of the cursor and insertion position to be specified. Note that the row number is specified first, followed by column number. The postfix increment operator on i ensures that the following cursor placement continues at the next row.

The function printw() is the *curses* equivalent of the formatted printf() routine found in the *stdio* library.

Previously, an appropriate number of newline characters were printed to scroll the previous display off the screen. This is now unnecessary because an initial call to erase() blanks out the screen for a fresh start.

c. Reading commands

The modification to function readCommandsAndInterpret only affects how the prompt is delivered and more importantly, how the single-key command is read. The code within the switch statement to interpret a command and act on it remains unchanged.

```
void readCommandsAndInterpret()
{
  int finish = 0;
  char c;

  while (!finish) {
    display(LINES-1);
    move(LINES-1, 0);
    standout();
    addstr("n)ext page p)revious page q)uit");
    standend();
    refresh();
    c = getch();
    switch (c) {
      /* similarly interpret command characters as before,
         and perform appropriate action */
    }
  }
}
```

As with the function display(), cursor movement and character display are handled by move() and addstr() respectively. The prompt is emphasized via calls to standout() and standend(). The *curses* function standout() causes subsequent character output to be highlighted. The complementary function standend() turns off highlighting and reverts to the normal display mode.

The view on the screen is completed when file contents and the prompt have been output via display() and addstr() respectively. The function refresh() is almost always invoked before reading the next command character so that the screen may be physically updated according to the change in the virtual screen as maintained by *curses*.

d. Program initialisation

Appropriate *curses* data structures are initialised via initscr() before calls to all other *curses* routines. Similarly, endwin() is invoked to reset terminal settings before exiting a program.

For the convenience of the browser user, each character is read in immediately. Thus, keyboard characters need not be echoed. These are reflected in the function main():

```
main(int argc, char **argv)
{
  FILE *fd;

  if (argc == 1) {
    printf("usage: %s file\n", argv[0]);
    exit(1);
  }
  fd = fopen(argv[1], "r");
  if (fd == NULL) {
    printf("%s: cannot open %s\n", argv[0], argv[1]);
    exit(1);
  }
  readFile(fd);
  fclose(fd);
  home();
  initscr();
  noecho();
  cbreak();
  readCommandsAndInterpret();
  endwin();
  exit(0);
}
```

4. 4   Linking Object Modules with Libraries

Libraries are precompiled code and suitable for linkage with various other modules. The inclusion of the "curses.h" header file merely causes interface information to be included for compile-time checks. As mentioned earlier, such header files typically contain external declarations.

References within a source file to library entities result in external references. The linker must resolve these to the corresponding public entries in the actual library.

Since UNIX compilers usually combine the tasks of compiling and linking, those flags not recognised as compiler flags are given to the linker. Libraries are specified via "-lx" to instruct the linker to use the library /usr/lib/lib$x$.a. Alternative library paths may be specified via "-Ly" so that a subsequent option "-lz" instructs the linker to use y/lib$z$.a if one exists.

Since the *curses* library already includes the *termcap* library, the latter need not be specified to the linker. Thus, the version of the browser which uses the *curses* library may be compiled and linked via:

```
$ gcc -o browser1 browser1.c -lcurses
```

4. 5   Other *curses* Features

We have only discussed basic *curses* functionalities. The *curses* library also allows for multiple windows, recognising function keys and key bindings, and a more elaborate screen attributes scheme.

a. Logical windows

The *curses* library actually allows for multiple logical windows. Each logical window maintains an associated set of data structures to represent its contents and state. A window is created via newwin() by specifying its size in terms of the number of lines and columns, and its upper left-hand corner coordinate y,x with respect to the physical screen. newwin() returns a reference to a newly created descriptor. All subsequent operations on the new window are made through this descriptor. It is subsequently destroyed via delwin():

```
WINDOW *newwin(int nlines, int ncols, int y, int x);
void delwin(WINDOW *win);
```

The *curses* library provides a corresponding set of functions to operate on user-created windows. These have similar functionality to those described earlier, except for an additional WINDOW parameter to specify the particular window involved.

```
void waddch(WINDOW *win, char);
void waddstr(WINDOW *win, char *);
void wprintw(WINDOW *win, char *, ...);
void wmove(WINDOW *win, int y, int x);
void wstandout(WINDOW *win);
void wstandend(WINDOW *win);

void werase(WINDOW *win);
void wclrtoeol(WINDOW *win);
void wclrtobot(WINDOW *win);

void wrefresh(WINDOW *win);
int  wgetch(WINDOW *win);
```

The default window stdscr is created during an initialisation call to initscr(). It has the same dimensions as the physical screen. In fact, functions which operate on stdscr, such as addch(x), are all implemented by calling the w versions with the stdscr window, e.g. waddch(stdscr,x).

b. Function keys

The character sequences sent by keypad and function keys may also be encoded in the *termcap* database. The input routines in *curses* cater for two modes of reading function keys: When the keypad mode is off, the input routines return the individual characters which are sent for each function key. When the keypad mode is on, the input routines return an encoding to represent the function key.

This is another example of how the *curses* library promotes terminal independence. As long as the physical key sequences generated by function keys are specified in the *termcap* entry, the getch() routine converts such representation into a logical key encoding.

The keypad mode is associated with a windows descriptor and the function keypad() turns the mode on with x=TRUE, and off with x=FALSE:

```
keypad(WINDOWS *win, bool x);
```

Function keys recognised by *curses* are given character encodings of 0401 (octal) and above. (As such, values cannot be stored in char variables.) A few encodings are reproduced in Table 4-2. It is often more convenient to use the symbolic name rather than the numeric encoding.

Key description	*curses* **encoding**	*curses* **symbolic name**
down arrow key	0402	KEY_DOWN
up arrow key	0403	KEY_UP
left arrow key	0404	KEY_LEFT
right arrow key	0405	KEY_RIGHT
F0 function key	0410	KEY_F0
Fn function key	0410+n	KEY_F(n)

Table 4-2: Sample of symbolic names of function keys

A full list is given in the *curses* interface file /usr/include/curses.h, as well as in the terminfo(4) manual page on file formats.

c. Forced updates

We have discussed the *curses* strategy where the virtual-window operators merely modify appropriate data structures. The refresh() function compares differences in views and writes the differences to update the terminal screen. This optimisation implies that nothing will be written to a terminal screen if `refresh()` is invoked without changes in the window contents.

The *curses* library provides the function `touchwin()` to indicate that nothing should be assumed about the existing view on the terminal screen. Thus, on the next `refresh()` call, the complete view is rewritten on the terminal screen.

```
void touchwin(WINDOW *win);
```

The screen must be redrawn for the following situations:

- Many interactive applications provide a screen redraw feature for occasions when the user's terminal screen is messed up due to a message by another user. Similarly, a mail arrival notice from the `biff` program easily messes up an interactive session, e.g. `vi`.

- Many interactive applications also provide suspend or escape-to-shell features. The suspend feature is part of job control facilities offered by later versions of UNIX. In this situation, an application hibernates until a resumption signal is received. When it can continue, it would want to redraw its screen because the contents of the screen cannot be assumed. The escape-to-shell situation is similar: here the application waits for the child shell process to terminate. When it does, it redraws the screen before continuing.

- For an interactive application which uses overlapping windows, a consistent window might be covered by another. A window brought to the top must be redrawn.

The function `redraw()` might be implemented via:

```
void redraw(WINDOW *win)
{
    touchwin(win);
    wrefresh(win);
}
```

d. Screen attributes

So far, we have only seen `standout()` and `standend()` for manipulating character attributes. The `attron()` and `attroff()` functions offer more general attributes for characters written by `addch()`, `addstr()` and `printw()`.

```
int attrset(int attrs);
int attroff(int attrs);
int attron(int attrs);
```

Attributes may be set with `attrset()` using values in Table 4-3, or combinations of them via a bitwise OR | operator:

A_STANDOUT	Best highlighting mode of the terminal
A_UNDERLINE	Underlining
A_REVERSE	Reverse video
A_BLINK	Blinking
A_DIM	Half bright
A_BOLD	Bold
A_NORMAL	Normal

Table 4-3: Screen attributes

The following code fragment

```
void attributes()
{
    attrset(A_NORMAL);
    printw("Normal\n");
    attrset(A_BOLD);
    printw("Bold\n");
    attrset(A_UNDERLINE);
    printw("Underlined\n");
    attrset(A_BOLD|A_UNDERLINE);
    printw("Bold and underlined\n");
}
```

produces

```
Normal
Bold
Underlined
Bold and underlined
```

The functions `attron()` and `attroff()` are used to turn on and off specific attributes, without affecting other attribute settings. Thus, `attron(A_BOLD)` and `attron(A_UNDERLINE)` result in both bold and underlined characters.

Often, `standout()` and `standend()` are implemented by calls to `attron(A_STANDOUT)` and `attroff(A_STANDOUT)` respectively. In addition, the following w functions are equivalent to those above, but with the extra window argument:

```
int wattrset(WINDOW *win, int attrs);
int wattroff(WINDOW *win, int attrs);
int wattron(WINDOW *win, int attrs);
```

e. Line editing

The functions `insch()` and `delch()` allow for limited forms of line editing.

```
void insch(chtype ch);
void delch();
```

The function `insch()` shifts the character at the current cursor position, and those to its right, by one column to the right. It then inserts character `ch` into the current cursor position.

The function `delch()` performs the complementary function of deleting the character at the current cursor position. All characters to the right of the cursor position are shifted by one column to the left.

4. 6   Summary

This chapter illustrates how an application might use an existing set of library routines. The *curses* library also gives a glimpse into the designing of modular interfaces, code reusability and hiding of implementation details (the implementation of `refresh()` is presumably complex, but understanding it is not important to using the library).

Functions in the *curses* library may be classified as follows:

§   initialisation and finalisation

```
initscr(), endwin()
```

§   writing output

```
addch(), addstr(), printw()
```

§   selective screen erase

```
erase(), clrtoeol(), clrtobot()
```

§   cursor placement

```
move()
```

§   line editing

```
insch(), delch()
```

§   setting character attributes

```
standout(), standend()
attrset(), attron(), attroff()
```

§   reading input

```
getch()
cbreak(), nocbreak(), echo(), noecho()
keypad()
```

§   Screen updating

```
refresh(), touchwin()
```

There are actually more *curses* facilities and their interface specifications are fully described in man curses.

4.7   Exercises

1. Provide the browser with a search facility. If it is helpful, change the display context such that the line containing the searched target is displayed in the middle of the screen. In addition, highlight the target string for clarity.

2. Implement a few trivial functions and make libraries of your own via the commands

```
gcc -c f1.c
gcc -c f2.c
ar q libmine.a f1.o f2.o
```

Refer to the library routines in another source file and produce an appropriate executable file. Find out if the order in which libraries occur in the command line is significant.

5

C Syntax and Semantics

We have now seen a fair amount of C code fragments and developed some appreciation of the run-time organisation of C programs. In addition, we have also gained some insight into the software development environment by building and extending a simple browser program.

It is now appropriate to consider the semantics of each construct in greater detail. In this chapter, we will examine C constructs systematically: definitions, expressions, control-flow statements, function scopes and parameters.

5. 1   Definitions

A C source program consists of a series of variable and function definitions. In the process of translation, a variable definition ultimately corresponds to a storage allocation. In turn, a variable reference becomes an access to the corresponding memory location. With regards to variable definitions, C also provides facilities for defining new structured types to model the problem domain. However, these type definitions do not cause any storage allocation since they merely specify the form of a variable in a subsequent definition. Storage allocation is only necessary for variable instances of such types.

A function definition also implies some form of storage allocation. In this case, some memory region must be set aside for the corresponding machine code generated when the function body is compiled. Ultimately, a function call becomes a branch instruction to that code region.

A function body is merely a statement block. It consists of local-data definitions and statements. Local-data definitions have forms similar to those of global definitions. As seen earlier, however, they require a different storage-allocation strategy.

5. 2   Variable Definitions

A variable definition has the basic form:

```
type-specifier name;
```

The simplest type specifiers are the predefined types such as character, integer and floating types: char, int and float. The following defines x to be an integer variable:

```
int x;
```

Since a list of names is also allowed, the following defines y and z to be character variables:

```
char y, z;
```

5. 3   Structured Variables

The definition of a variable of a structured type is similar to that of a predefined type. The *type-specifier* either denotes a composite-record type, or a union type.

a. Record variables

The specification of a record type is elaborate because the notation must allow for field names and associated types. Fortunately, the definition of fields is very similar to that for variables. A record specifier has the form:

```
struct record-name {
    type-specifier field-name;
    . . .
};
```

A record variable r of type struct t with two fields f and g may be defined as follows:

```
struct t {
   int f;
   char *g;
};
struct t r;
```

If r is the only instance of type struct t, the notations may be merged to:

```
struct t {
   int f;
   char *g;
} r;
```

Access to a field must be qualified by the record variable via the standard dot . notation. The field g of record variable r is referenced via:

```
r.g
```

b. Union variables

The usage of a set of variables is sometimes disjointed: if w is used, v is not required, and vice versa. It follows that this set of variables may be defined within a union type as:

```
union u {
   int w;
   char *v;
} s;
```

The syntax of the union type resembles that of the struct type, but their semantics differ drastically. The memory allocation required to hold values of a struct type is the sum of the requirements of its individual fields. However, disjoint usage of union members allow them to be allocated the same memory region. The memory requirement to a union variable is then that of the largest member.

As with struct types, access to a member is qualified by the union variable. It should be noted that there is no tag facility to distinguish which union member was most recently assigned. In the case of union variable x above, accessing v after assigning to w merely returns the residual value of an integer interpreted as a character pointer.

This situation should be avoided. The results are implementation dependent, and as such, cannot be assumed for a different environment or target platform. An additional programmer-defined tag to track the legitimate value is highly recommended.

5. 4   Declarators

Pointers, arrays and functions are defined using declarators with symbols *, [] and ()
respectively. Thus, the more accurate form for variable definitions should be:

```
type-specifier declarator, declarator...;
```

As we saw previously with the definition of variables, a name is the simplest declarator. The
notation of a declarator is such that when it appears in an expression, it refers to an object with
the same type specifier as indicated at its definition.

For the sake of comparison, notice that in Pascal, a pointer to some type T is denoted
by augmenting the type name to ^T. However, the declarator notation in C augments the
variable name instead.

a. Pointer variables

Pointer variables are often preceded by the indirection operator "*". For the following
definition, the declarator notation makes *pi an integer variable, in the same way that i is
defined to be an integer variable:

```
int *pi;
int i;
```

Since *pi is an integer, this makes pi a pointer to an integer. (While int* pi is syntactically
equivalent and is an acceptable formatting convention for defining pointer variables, it is not
encouraged. The *prefix* indirection operator "*" applies to the right operand; in this case, pi
and not int.)

Since the prefix indirection operator "*" binds to the right operand, the following
definition does **not** correctly define p1 and p2 as character pointers:

```
char* p1, p2;
```

Instead, p1 and p2 are only character pointers if *p1 and *p2 are character variables, just as y
and z were previously defined as character variables. Thus, character pointers p1 and p2 must
instead be defined as:

```
char *p1, *p2;
```

b. Array variables

Array elements are accessed by the subscript operator `[]`. It follows that the following definition makes each element `a[i]` an integer variable, and thus defines `a` to be an integer array:

```
int a[20];
```

The constant expression defines the size of the array. In C, array subscripts always start with 0. Thus, the 20 elements of the array are accessed via `a[0]`, `a[1]`, `a[2]`, ..., `a[18]` and finally, `a[19]`.

The notation for multidimension arrays is similar: the following definition makes each element `b[i][j]` a float variable. As with `a` above, each element `b[i]` is then a float array. Thus, `b` is defined to be a two-dimensional float array.

```
float b[20][30];
```

Unlike Pascal, the name of an array in an expression in C does not represent its contents. Instead, an array name returns the address of its first element. As illustrated in the fragment below, the name of an array with elements of `T` is compatible with a pointer-to-`T` variable.

```
float c[10];
float *d;

d = c;
```

Since the name `c` returns the address of its first element, assigning it to `d` will make `d` reference the same location. As such, both `c[0]` and `*d` return the value of the first element.

In general, the address of `c[n]` is obtained by `address(c)+n*sizeof(float)`. However, that element may also be accessed via `*(c+n)`, or `*(d+n)`. The reader might be surprised to note that the size of the array element is not taken into consideration. However, pointer arithmetic (the values of pointers `c` and `d` are in fact addresses) in C is in terms of storage units of the type referenced by the pointer. Thus, the multiplication of `sizeof(float)` is already implied by address addition. In this respect, `d[n]` also returns the same array element.

While `c` and `d` might appear to have similar usage, they are different in that `c` cannot be assigned:

```
c = d;
```

This is reasonable, as the pointer d may be made to reference the base of array c; but as array c is already allocated memory, it cannot be moved to the location referenced by d.

c. Function declarations

We recall that we inferred previously the definition of pi as an integer pointer variable because applying the indirection operator "*" to pi returns an integer:

```
int *pi;
```

Similarly, the following code fragment declares f to be a function that returns an integer, because f() in an expression denotes a function call which returns an integer result:

```
int f();
```

It is logical that the following declares g to be a function that accepts an integer argument and returns a float result:

```
float g(int);
```

Note that a function declaration, as with f or g, (as opposed to a function definition) merely describes interface information and states how it might be used. Thus, no code is generated for a function declaration, since it serves as a compile-time facility. This information is recorded in the symbol table so that usage may be checked for consistency.

Such declarations are useful for mutually recursive functions (where the definition might occur later in the source file), or when the function is to be defined in another program file. In addition, function declarations can be used as interface specifications when designing modular structure.

Code generation only occurs for the body of function definitions. We will discuss these in subsequent sections.

d. Combining declarators

The three declarator forms described earlier allow for limited combinations. This provides for a flexible and rich set of data structures. For example, the following code fragment defines m as a 25-element array of character pointers, while n is a function which accepts an integer argument and returns a character pointer.

```
char *m[25];
char *n(int);
```

Unlike Pascal, C allows the address of a function to be assigned to a variable. Such functions may subsequently be invoked via the indirection operator. The syntax for pointers to functions follow naturally from the combination of declarators. Recall that a function like `factorial` which accepts an integer parameter and returns an integer result may be declared as:

```
int factorial(int);
```

It follows that pointer `p` to such a function which accepts an integer parameter and returns an integer would be defined as:

```
int (*p)(int);
```

The importance of type consistency is evident here. Only the address of a function with interface specifications similar to that of the function pointer `p` may be assigned to it. If this were not so, inappropriate parameters would be supplied to the function when it is invoked indirectly.

Note that a function name on its own denotes the address of the function. This is distinct from a function call, which is denoted with parentheses, for example, `factorial(5)`. Thus, the following assignment copies the address of function `factorial` to variable `p`:

```
p = factorial;
```

Calling function `factorial(5)` is hence the same as `(*p)(5)`. Note, too, that the declarations for function `n` and function pointer `p` above differ only by an extra set of parentheses. Function invocation "`()`" has a higher precedence than the indirection operator "`*`". Therefore, `*z()` is interpreted as `*(z())` and not `(*z)()`. Parentheses are used to override precedence rules if the semantics of `p` were intended instead.

Similarly, `char *m[25]` differs from `char (*q)[25]`. `m` is an array of 25 character pointers, but `q` is a pointer to a 25-character array. Again, the subscript operator "`[]`" has a higher precedence than the indirection operation "`*`"; and `*m[x]` is interpreted as `*(m[x])`. The extra parentheses, as with `q`, binds "`*`" to itself, making `q` a pointer, but `m` an array.

However, not all declarator combinations are allowable. Restrictions include:

- Arrays, `struct` or `union` instances may not be functions (though pointers to functions are permissible);

- Functions may not return structured items such as arrays, structs or unions, or other functions (though pointers to such items are permissible).

5. 5   Type Declarations

The data-structuring facilities (structs and unions) and use of declarators ([], * and ()) allow for flexible usage combinations to conveniently model the problem domain. However, when the same structures are required in various program fragments, it might be tedious to repeat such declarations.

Instead of repeating the various structures or declarator forms throughout the program source, it is more convenient to declare a form and associate it with a type name. The notations used for type declarations are similar to variable declarations, but prefixed with the typedef keyword. The following fragment shows this similarity. It defines pi as an integer pointer, and makes tpi a type synonym for integer pointers.

```
int *pi;
typedef int *tpi;
```

Subsequently, the following definition defines pia and pib as integer pointer variables:

```
tpi pia, pib;
```

Type names are aliases in that they provide another means of referring to the type in question. In the above example, tpi is another name for an integer pointer, and does not declare a new type.

5. 6   Statements and Expressions

As in most high-level languages, statements in C may be grouped into

- simple statements, which are not composed from other statements, and

- structured statements, which contain other statements in its body.

The most common simple statements are expression statements, which include assignments and function calls. Others include the goto, break and continue statements.

Structured statements are control constructs which determine whether and how the statements in its body are executed. These include the if and if-else conditional statements, and while, while-do and for iterative constructs.

a. Expression statement

An expression statement is merely an expression, which by the trailing semicolon, has been elevated to the category of a statement. It may thus occur in the context of a statement, such as:

```
a;
a+b;
areaOfTriangle(a,b);
```

Note that in the context of procedural languages, the above C expression statements are legal. However, they are not significant since they do not produce any side-effect such as the updating of a variable, nor are their results used. This includes the function `areaOfTriangle()` shown below. It returns a result, but without any side-effect:

```
int areaOfTriangle(int base, int height)
{
    return(base*height/2);
}
```

Recall that programs based on the Von Neumann model compute answers by making incremental updates on its states. In the cases above, there is no such side-effect.

Since the assignment operator "=" in C produces a side-effect, it is about the most commonly used expression statement. It accepts a reference to an object on its left and alters its value to that returned by the expression on the right:

```
v = e;
```

Being an operator (just as "+" is an operator), it also returns a result; in this case, the value assigned. Semantically, it is therefore legal to use this result as an operand for another expression. Of course, this expression could be used within another assignment, such as:

```
x = y = 0;
```

The assignment operator associates from right to left, and thus y is assigned before x. In practice, we should be careful about mixing assignments with expression evaluation because of the subtle but real potential problems of side-effects and the order of evaluation. The following is one such example where one might be uncertain as to whether 10 was assigned to a[8] or a[9][1]:

```
i = 8;
j = (a[i] = 10) + (i = 9);
```

The left-hand side operand of an assignment is also historically known as an *lvalue*. It denotes the storage location allocated to a variable and thus represents a reference to a destination object which receives a new value. Since an array name represents the base address of the array and not a location to store a value, it cannot be used as the left-hand side operand of an assignment operator.

b. Expression forms

The simplest expression is a primary expression, which consists of a literal, variable name, function call, array element or record field. These are enumerated in Table 5-1.

Primary-Expn	Example	Remarks
literal	3 0x435f 037 10.4 'a' "hi there\n"	integer constant hexadecimal constant octal constant floating pointer constant character constant string
identifier	count	variable reference
primary-expn **(** *expression-list* **)**	factorial(4)	function call
primary-expn **[** *expression* **]**	group[i]	array subscript
lvalue **.** *identifier*	person.age	struct field
primary-expn **->** *identifier*	p->age	field access via pointer to struct
(*expression* **)**	(*p).age	() can alter evaluation order

Table 5-1: Simple expressions

The recursive definition of an expression involving unary, binary or ternary operators allow for more complex forms. These notations are summarised in Table 5-2.

---

[1] The C reference manual does not specify the evaluation order for operands of a commutative operator.

Expression	Example	Remarks
primary-expn		as summarised in previous table
* *expression*	`*p`	indirection: returns the *lvalue* of the object pointed to by `p`
& *lvalue*	`&q`	address-of (complement of indirection): returns the address of object `q`
– *expression*	`-a`	arithmetic negation: returns `-5` if `a` has value `5`
! *expression*	`!a`	logical negation: returns `1/0` if `a` is `0/1`
~ *expression*	`~a`	one's complement: returns value with complement bits of `a`
++*lvalue*	`++m`	prefix increment: increments `m`, and returns its new value
– –*lvalue*	`--n[a]`	prefix decrement: decrements `n[a]`, and returns its new value
*lvalue***++**	`m++`	postfix increment: increments `m`, but returns its original value
*lvalue***– –**	`n[a]--`	postfix decrement: decrements `n[a]`, but returns its original value
sizeof (*expression* **)**	`sizeof(a)`	size of object: returns allocation of `a`
(*type-name* **)** *expression*	`(int *) a`	type casting: treat the value of `a` as an integer pointer
expression ***** *expression*	`a * b`	multiplication: returns `a*b`
expression **/** *expression*	`a / b`	division: returns `a/b`
expression **%** *expression*	`a % b`	modulus: returns `a` mod `b`
expression **+** *expression*	`a + b`	addition: returns `a+b`
expression **–** *expression*	`a - b`	subtraction: returns `a-b`
expression **>>** *expression*	`a >> b`	bit shift: returns `a` shifted right by `b`
expression **<<** *expression*	`a << b`	bit shift: returns `a` shifted left by `b`
expression **<** *expression*	`a < b`	less: returns `1` if `a` is less than `b`
expression **>** *expression*	`a > b`	greater: returns `1` if `a` is greater than `b`
expression **<=** *expression*	`a <= b`	less or equal: returns `1` if `a` is greater than `b`
expression **>=** *expression*	`a >= b`	greater or equal: returns `1` if `a` is greater than `b`
expression **==** *expression*	`a == b`	equality: returns `1` if `a` is equal to `b`
expression **!=** *expression*	`a != b`	inequality: returns `1` if `a` is not equal to `b`

Expression	Example	Remarks
expression **&** *expression*	a & b	bitwise AND
expression **^** *expression*	a ^ b	bitwise exclusive OR
expression **|** *expression*	a | b	bitwise inclusive OR
expression **&&** *expression*	a && b	logical AND
expression **||** *expression*	a || b	logical OR
expression **?** *expression* : *expression*	a ? b : c	conditional expression: return b if a is nonzero, else c
lvalue **=** *expression*	a = b + 1	assignment: a gets b+1, returns a
lvalue **+=** *expression*	a += g-4	a = a+(g-4)
lvalue **-=** *expression*		variants: x op= y to mean
lvalue ***=** *expression*		x = x op (y)
lvalue **/=** *expression*		
lvalue **%=** *expression*		
lvalue **>>=** *expression*		
lvalue **<<=** *expression*		
lvalue **&=** *expression*		
lvalue **^=** *expression*		
lvalue **|=** *expression*		
expression **,** *expression*	a+1, b+2	expression list: evaluates a+1 for side-effects, returns b+2

Table 5-2: Expressions and operators

An operator which causes a side-effect must refer to objects. Thus, it requires *lvalue* operands. These include the assignment operator with its variants, as well as the increment/decrement operators. The address-of & operator returns the address of an object, and thus requires an *lvalue* operand too. Excluding literals and function calls, most primary expressions are *lvalue* operands and are enumerated in Table 5-3.

lvalue
identifier
primary-expn **[** *expression* **]**
lvalue **.** *identifier*
primary-expn **->** *identifier*
(*lvalue* **)**
* *expression*

Table 5-3: Variable references

c. Operator precedence and associativity rules

Since structured statements merely direct how their statement bodies execute, expression statements ultimately form the fundamental workhorse for computing and moving values about in C programs. However, the informal set of specifications for nested expressions, as in the previous tables, is still ambiguous and inadequate for interpreting and translating C programs. For example, two abstract syntax trees exist for the expression:

```
*name[i]
```

It could be interpreted as:

```
*(name[i])     or     (*name)[i]
```

C resolves such ambiguities via *operator precedence* and *associativity* rules. They are important in C because of the vast number of operators.

Operator precedence provides a scale of how strongly an operator, in relation to another, binds to operands. In the previous example, the first interpretation of the original expression is adopted if the subscript operator "[]" has a higher precedence to bind stronger than indirection "*". The second interpretation of the original expression would be adopted only if the indirection "*" operator binds tighter than the subscript operator "[]".

An ambiguity then persists when two operators have equal precedence, such as

```
*p++
```

Here, the increment "++" and indirection "*" operators have the same precedence level. For situations where precedence is not useful in resolving the ambiguity, associativity rules are used instead. In this case, the two interpretations (*p)++ and *(p++) result from left-to-right and right-to-left associativity respectively.

Table 5-4 gives the precedence and associativity of C operators. Operator precedence is first used to resolve any ambiguity. If this is not helpful, associativity rules are used.

	Operator	Associativity
highest precedence	`() [] . ->`	left-to-right
	`*`(*indirect*) `&`(*addr*) `- ! ~ ++ -- sizeof` (*type-name*)	right-to-left
	`* / %`	left-to-right
	`+ -`	left-to-right
	`>> <<`	left-to-right
	`< > <= >=`	left-to-right
	`== !=`	left-to-right
	`&`	left-to-right
	`^`	left-to-right
	`|`	left-to-right
	`&&`	left-to-right
	`||`	left-to-right
	`? :`	left-to-right
	`= += -= *= /= %= >>= <<= &= ^= |=`	right-to-left
lowest precedence	`,`	left-to-right

Table 5-4: Operator precedence and associativity

5. 7   Control-flow Constructs

Control-flow constructs are used to modify the execution order of expression statements. Structured constructs comprise conditional and iterative constructs. A conditional construct allows the selection of one of its statement bodies to be executed; whereas an iterative construct allows its body to be executed a number of times. These constructs may be augmented by branch statements in situations where it is more natural to express the program structure in such a way.

a. `if-else` statement

The `if-else` conditional construct allows for the selection of execution paths. It has the following form, with the `else` part optional:

```
if (expression)
    statement₁
else
    statement₂
```

The conditional *expression* is first evaluated. If it returns a non-zero value (indicating true), `statement₁` is executed. If it is a zero value (indicating false), `statement₂` is executed.

Since statement parts may further contain a nested `if-else` statement, the ambiguity of a dangling `else` part is solved by binding it to the most recent `if` part. Alternatively, a compound statement block may be used to make the structure explicit. While the syntax differs from the Pascal `if-then-else` statement, the semantics of the two are identical.

b. Compound block

A compound statement block denoted by { } delimiters may occur anywhere a statement is expected and has the effect of a single statement.

This facility for sequencing and abstraction is quite similar to the `begin-end` compound statement in Pascal. However, the block in C is more general in that it allows for local variable definitions, just as in the body of a function definition.

c. while statement

The `while` statement is a pretest condition-controlled iterative construct. It has the form:

```
while (expression)
    statement
```

The conditional `expression` is first evaluated. If it returns a non-zero value, the `statement` body is executed, followed by the conditional `expression` again. The cycle continues until the `expression` returns a zero value, at which point control transfers to after `statement`. As with the `if-else` statement, the syntax might differ from the Pascal `while` statement, but again, the semantics of the `while` statements are identical.

d. for statement

The `for` statement in C is another iterative construct. However, it is drastically different from the Pascal `for` statement. The latter is a counter-controlled iterative construct, where an explicit loop variable exists and is either automatically incremented or decremented. The former, however, does not have such characteristics. Instead it is basically a pretest condition-controlled loop with initialisation and reinitialisation code fragments.

```
for (statement_init; expression; statement_reinit)
    statement
```

Its form above is easily transformed into something equivalent and more familiar:

```
statement_init;
while (expression) {
    statement
    statement_reinit;
}
```

Note that the semicolons delimit the three code fragments. They are mandatory even if one of `statement_init`, `expression`, or `statement_reinit` is empty. When `expression` is empty, the loop condition is taken to be always non-zero, and would thus behave as an "infinite" loop. In this case, it is assumed that there are other means to break out of the loop.

```
for (i = 1; i<=10; i++) {
    ...a[i]
}
```

The `for` counter-controlled loop in Pascal may be simulated as in the above code fragment. The terminating condition compares the implied loop index variable against the upper bound. However, it is also common to use a less-than operator since array indices range from 0 to $n-1$ (n being the size of the array).

```
#define   MAX   25
int a[MAX];

for (i = 0; i<MAX; i++)
    a[i] = 0;
```

e. do-while statement

Finally, the `do-while` construct is a post-test condition-controlled loop with the form

```
do statement while (expression);
```

It is similar to the `while` construct except that the conditional expression is evaluated after executing the statement part. The body of a pre-test condition-controlled loop is executed zero or more times, the body of a post-test condition-controlled loop is executed one or more times. This is somewhat similar to the `repeat-until` construct in Pascal.

f. break and continue statements

Two other statements are used with iterative constructs: the break and continue statements. The break statement causes the *enclosing* iterative construct to be terminated so that control is transferred to immediately after the loop. This is a means to break out of an iterative construct whose condition is always *true*.

The continue statement has a similar function to the break statement, but only terminates the current iteration by branching to the end of the statement body. For the while and do-while constructs, the conditional expression will thus be evaluated to determine if looping will continue. In the case of the for construct, the reinitialisation statement is executed before determining if looping will continue. In this respect, the for statement to while statement transformation suggested earlier is not totally accurate.

The use of the break and continue statements are in principle unnecessary, since the same effect may be achieved by augmenting the conditional expression and/or an additional test. The decision as to the best program structure is context dependent, and is left to the programmer.

g. switch statement

The switch construct in C allows for a multi-way selection of statement bodies. It is similar to the case statement in standard Pascal, with the exception that the former

- does not have implicit branching out after each statement limb, and

- has a default limb so as to catch cases where the switch expression does not match any labels.

It has the general form:

```
switch (expression) {
   case v₁: s₁;
   case v₂: s₂;
            break;
   case vₖ: sₖ;
            break;
   ...
   default: sₐ;
            break;
}
```

The break statement has an additional use in that it skips out of a switch limb. When the evaluation of *expression* returns a constant value v_1, the corresponding statement s_1 is executed. The absence of an implicit branch after statement s_1 causes execution to proceed to statement s_2. However, following the execution of s_k, the `break` statement causes control to transfer to after the `switch` statement.

h. goto statement

Lastly, all statements may be optionally prefixed by label identifiers. Unlike Pascal, labels in C look like identifiers. The `goto` statement allows branching to a local label site (within the function body). While C does not have non-local branches, a restricted form is discussed in chapter 10.

5.8   Function Definitions

A function definition is obtained by augmenting a function prototype declaration with a function body containing implementation code. A function body is merely a compound statement block consisting of a statement sequence optionally preceded by local variable definitions. It has the following form:

```
return-type-specifier name ( formal-parameters-type-list )
{
    local-definitions
    statement-list
}
```

Local variable definitions are similar to that of global definitions which we saw earlier. They have similar semantics, referencing and access mechanisms. Their scope and lifetime are however restricted to the function in which they are declared. They have the following properties:

- The scope of a local variable is limited to the block it was defined in, and any nested block which does not contain another definition for the same name. This is consistent with abstraction principles.

- The lifetime of a variable is the time-span in which it is allocated storage. This corresponds to the time that the block in which it is defined is active. It translates to the time when a block is invoked, up to when control returns to its caller.

As an example, a function to sum the first *n* natural numbers might be defined as follows:

```
int sumTo(int n)
{
    int x;

    x = 0;
    while (n > 0) {
        x = x+n;
        n = n-1;
    }
    return(x);
}
```

A function call involves binding the formal parameters to actual values and executing the compound statement corresponding to the function body.

The `return` statement terminates execution of a function and thus returns control to the caller. Where a return type is included in the function specification, an appropriate return result is expected. In this case, the value is returned via the `return` statement.

A function which is not expected to return any value terminates via a null return statement or after executing the last statement of the function body.

5.9   Parameter Passing

A parameter-passing mechanism promotes the reusability of functions. The mechanism provided in C is known as *pass-by-value*. It is similar to the default parameter-passing mode in Pascal and is graphically illustrated in Figure 5-1.

As the name implies, a function allocates sufficient storage in its parameter area to receive **values** from its caller. Such parameters are accessed and manipulated via the formal parameter names. In this respect, formal parameters might be thought of as similar local variables, except that they have pre-initialised values. Since a function manipulates its own storage areas, the actual parameters in such cases would be unaffected by the manipulation of parameters from within the function. Consequently, pass-by-value parameters may be thought of as an input parameter mechanism for a black-box machine.

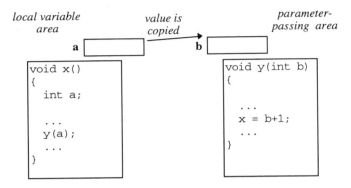

Figure 5-1: Implementation of a pass-by-value parameter

An output parameter mechanism is implied when manipulations performed within a function must be reflected in the actual parameters. Here, Pascal relies on pass-by-reference parameters or **var** parameters. In this case, instead of transmitting a value, the caller passes the address of the actual parameter. A function then allocates storage in its parameter area for the address of the variable to be manipulated, as shown in Figure 5-2. Access and modification of the actual parameters would thus require an extra level of indirection.

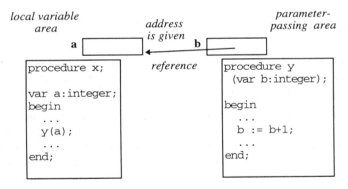

Figure 5-2: Implementation of a pass-by-reference parameter

The mechanics of parameter passing-by-reference is fully supported by the Pascal implementation because it is a language feature. While it is necessary to have an output parameter mechanism, C does not have pass-by-reference parameters formally defined in the language. However, the basic language facilities allow pass-by-reference parameters to be manually prescribed by the programmer. This is achieved by the use of the address-of "&" and indirection "*" operators.

For example, the address of the actual parameter b may be passed to the function twoMore to increase its value by two via:

```
int b;

twoMore(&b);
```

The implementation of function twoMore() accesses and manipulates the actual parameter via an extra indirection (*m).

```
void twoMore(int *m)
{
    *m = *m + 2;
}
```

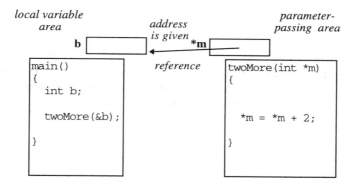

Figure 5-3: Parameter passing in C

5. 10   Type Casting

Type information is useful in a high-level language mainly because it allows for type-consistency checks to be performed at either compile time or run time. This helps in detecting programmer errors. Where the type is known, storage requirement may also be inferred, and thus can be performed automatically by the implementation.

Sometimes however, it might be convenient to bypass type restrictions. This can be achieved using explicit type conversion or type casting. While g is of type T below, it might be casted to type Q:

```
T g;
...
(Q) g
```

Type casting should be avoided as much as possible because it usually makes various assumptions about the internal representations adopted by a language implementation or a target machine. Program portability is a concern in this situation since these assumptions might not be valid for a different environment.

5. 11   Storage-class Specifiers

We have seen that the `typedef` keyword may precede a definition so that the name is treated as a type alias. Other storage-class specifiers that may precede definitions include `extern`, `static`, `register` and `auto`.

a. **extern** specifier

Variable and function *definitions* such as `b` and `twoMore` in the previous section serve two purposes. First, the compiler records that `b` is a variable of type `int`, and that `twoMore` is a function which is expecting an integer pointer parameter. This involves inserting appropriate symbol table entries at compile time when definitions are encountered, so that subsequent usage may be type-checked.

Second, storage must be allocated for the variable `b` so that it may store assigned values. Similarly, storage must also be allocated for the generated code corresponding to the function body of `twoMore`.

Such definitions must be contrasted with variable and function *declarations* which are preceded by an `extern` keyword:

```
extern int c;
extern int f();
int g();
```

Declarations merely serve the first purpose of compile-time information and consistency checking, but not the second purpose of storage allocation. Their usage is common with programs which span multiple files. In this case, `c` and `f()` are forward defined. That is to say, they are declared and referenced in advance of a definition. An appropriate definition must subsequently exist, either in the same program file or in another program file.

An `extern` keyword is assumed for all function declarations. As such, `extern` is already implied in the declaration of `g()`. Conversely, an `extern` keyword before a function definition is ignored since storage must be allocated for code generated from the analysis of the function body.

b. static specifier

By default, the linker advertises the name of every global variable and function definition. A declaration in a different program file, but with the same name, is ultimately mapped by the linker to the location associated with the definition. As such, there can only be one definition of a name, whether in the same program file, or another file that might subsequently be linked to form the system.

A global definition which is preceded by a static keyword is treated as private to the program file. In effect, it prevents the linker from using it as a public name during symbol resolution. No declaration will then be mapped to such definitions.

The static specifier is useful to entities whose scopes are strictly confined to the program file. It ensures that they will not interfere with entities in other program files.

c. auto specifier

Local variables are also known as automatic variables because they are allocated on function entry, and deallocated on function exit. This implies that for two recursive calls, a local variable will not be allocated the same storage location. Consequently, values of local variables are not retained across function calls.

On the other hand, the static keyword before a local variable overrides its default as an auto variable. Its effect is that while its scope is limited to the block, as with other local variables, it is allocated storage like global variables. A static variable is not allocated storage at run time, or even over recursive calls. Thus, static local variables retain their values across function calls.

d. register specifier

Lastly, a variable definition may be preceded by a register keyword. It is often used to indicate frequent access, and causes a register to be used to hold variable contents. However, since most compilers already perform some kind of register optimisation, programmer-specified register allocation might be counter-productive unless it is consistent with the underlying register allocation strategy already adopted by the compiler. It should thus be used prudently, and only after register allocation issues are fully understood.

5. 12   Independent Compilation

We have seen that the C code for an application may be logically partitioned into independent files. However, the file in which a variable or function definition occurs does not change the semantics of the program. For each variable definition, the compiler must allocate memory space in the data segment, regardless of the location of the definition. Similarly, it translates each function definition into its equivalent machine code and places the resultant into the code segment.

Where an appropriate external declaration exists, the type information allows the compiler to generate appropriate code but to leave an address placeholder in the incomplete machine code instruction. As we saw previously, this placeholder is subsequently replaced by an appropriate address at link time. By then, the addresses of all definitions must be known.

Independent compilation and the ultimate linking phase might thus cause variables and functions to be loaded at different places in the memory during run time as compared to when only one program file is used, but this does not alter the semantics of C facilities.

5. 13   Summary

This chapter has reviewed the basic building blocks of C programs. As with any language based on the Von Neumann model, C provides facilities for defining variables and manipulating their values. Like many high-level languages, facilities are also provided for defining new types from predefined building blocks.

Of equal importance is the large range of operators and control constructs in C. Operator precedence is important so that expressions have the intended semantics. This chapter has provided sufficient background to understand and use the mechanisms provided in C.

5. 14   Exercises

1. Tidy up the browser code by defining and using appropriate abstract data types.

2. The browser currently breaks up long lines so that they fit into the physical display area. Improve on the display strategy so that long lines are displayed appropriately. A popular scheme allows the terminal screen to act as a periscope which scans a wide virtual display area. The view of the periscope must then follow the area of focus as indicated by the cursor position.

3. Modify the browser to include simple editing facilities, like inserting and deleting characters within a line. Ensure that there is maximum reusability of code in that the

executables of the browser and editor can be generated from the same set of source files. (Note that following an insertion, the storage allocation for a line must be adjusted accordingly to accommodate extra characters.)

4. Extend on the functionality of the basic editor in question 3 by implementing the insertion and deletion of lines.

5. Implement a command look-up table so that command-key bindings may be user-defined at run time.

6

Making System Calls

An operating system manages hardware resources by sharing them fairly and efficiently amongst all users. Without an operating system, users might have to physically queue to use the system one at a time. Such a regime would be necessary to prevent undesirable interaction between users. Though crude, it avoids printer listings interspersed with output from different users.

In effect, an operating system provides each user with the full services of a virtual machine. Each user is allocated some processor time, memory space and device usage. A hard-disk device is used to implement a file system and each user is typically granted a portion of it. The operating system ensures that devices are shared consistently so that files or printouts from two users are not merged.

Since the operating system is custodian over all resources, each user program may use these resources only when requests are granted by the operating system. Note that an operating system cannot effectively implement its functions unless it is the sole custodian and has absolute control over all resources. If a program can use a resource without permission from the operating system, it is unlikely that the state maintained by the operating system is consistent. This implies that requests to the operating system must be appropriately validated. The security at the operating system interface must never be breached.

The interface to the UNIX operating system kernel is also known as the UNIX system calls. Since the kernel manages shared resources, integrity is maintained by allowing requests and usage of resources to take place only via the appropriate system calls, and then under appropriate circumstances. For example, requests to open and read a file will only be granted by the kernel if the file exists and the user has appropriate read permissions. Apart from such calls, there are no other means by which files, hard-disk devices or other share resources may be accessed and used by a user.

Library routines are somewhat related to system calls in that they are typically invoked by programs. However, while libraries might accompany a UNIX system, they are merely pre-compiled routines which have been found to be useful across a large range of application programs. As such, while some libraries are packaged with the operating system, it is not always the case. Since they are not privileged code, they may be implemented and packaged by users too.

6. 1   Notation and Documentation

The following chapters will examine various UNIX system calls and library routines more closely. The function prototype notation, as used for UNIX manual pages, is adopted. The succinct notation provides details about the parameters which must accompany each call. Where appropriate, header files are also specified because these contain related prototype information and associated parameters. These must be included in the program sources.

Just as UNIX commands are described in section 1 of the on-line UNIX manual pages, complete details of system calls and library routines may be found in sections 2 and 3 respectively. It is typically unnecessary to know where a particular manual description occurs because the man command sequentially searches for manual pages in each section. Thus, man ls prints out a description of the ls command, whereas man fork prints out a description of the fork() system call.

On occasions when manual entries in the various sections have the same name, only the first entry is printed. For example, sysinfo is both the name of the UNIX command and the corresponding system call to query system information. In such a case, the -s option in the man command overrides the sequential search through sections by indicating the section number explicitly. Thus, -s 2 is used to print out the manual page for the sysinfo() system call. The following output would be obtained in Solaris 2.3[1]:

---

[1] For other versions, the -s option is not required.

```
$ man -s 2 sysinfo
sysinfo(2)                    System Calls                    sysinfo(2)


NAME
     sysinfo - get and set system information strings

SYNOPSIS
     #include <sys/systeminfo.h>
     int sysinfo(int command, char *buf, int count);

DESCRIPTION
     sysinfo() copies information relating to the operating system
     on which the process is executing into the buffer pointed to by
     buf; sysinfo() can also set certain information where appropriate
     commands are available. count is the size of the buffer.

more...
```

The description format is fairly standard. For system and library calls, the NAME section gives the name of the item being described with a brief description of functionality. The SYNOPSIS section provides interface information in terms of suitable C function prototypes and appropriate interface .h files. The DESCRIPTION provides more details of the parameters and behaviour of the routine in question. The other three sections, RETURN VALUES, ERRORS and SEE ALSO provide a summary of results and error situations, together with cross-references.

The notation *name(n)* is often used in cross-references. It refers to the manual page for *name* in section *n*.

6.2   Making a System Call

A UNIX system call from a C program looks the same as a function call. A simple program to obtain and display system information could be implemented as in Listing 6-1.

```
#include <stdio.h>
#include <sys/systeminfo.h>

main()
{   char buffer[BUFSIZ];
    sysinfo(SI_HOSTNAME, buffer, BUFSIZ);
    printf("%s\n", buffer);
    exit(0);
}
```

Listing 6-1: Hostname program

Note that the formal parameter types as specified in the function prototype are matched by the actual parameters in the sample fragment. The symbolic constant SI_HOSTNAME and others are elaborated on in the DESCRIPTION section.

However, the above programming style is sloppy. The result of the system call should have been tested since there are many reasons why a call might not be successful. While the hostname of a system is almost always defined and thus obtainable, there is no guarantee of success. Program bugs are often the result of unexpected program conditions. Hence, it is always good practice to test the results of system calls.

We next consider the complement of SI_HOSTNAME: the command constant SI_SET_HOSTNAME which allows the system's hostname to be modified. Since it would be chaotic if each user changes the hostname at will, the operating system kernel ensures that only the system administrator is allowed such a privilege.

6. 3   Error Codes and Error Reporting

In general, system calls return the value -1 to indicate failure. Attempting to change the hostname of a system will return this result, unless the program in Listing 6-2 was executed by root or as root[2].

The most recent error code may be obtained via the external variable errno. This code may be used to index the external string array sys_errlist to obtain a concise description of the error situation. Error codes are further discussed in the intro(2) manual page. It would be more robust and helpful if such error conditions were detected and reported appropriately.

```
#include <stdio.h>
#include <sys/systeminfo.h>

main()
{   char buffer[BUFSIZ];

    if (sysinfo(SI_SET_HOSTNAME, buffer, strlen(buffer)+1) == -1) {
        extern int errno;
        extern char *sys_errlist[];
        printf("%s\n", sys_errlist[errno]);
        exit(1);
    }
    exit(0);
}
```

Listing 6-2: Set hostname program

---

[2] *setuid* and *setgid* programs are discussed in chapter 8.

The external variable `sys_nerr` contains the size of the `sys_errlist` array. It could be used to double-check that `errno` has a valid error code. Since error reporting occurs frequently, it is a good habit to adopt abstraction techniques. As shown below, we might package error-reporting code into a function `report_err()`:

```
void report_err(char *prefix)
{
    extern int errno;
    extern int sys_nerr;
    extern char *sys_errlist[];

    if (prefix != NULL)
        printf("%s: ", prefix);
    if (0 < errno && errno < sys_nerr)
        printf("%s\n", sys_errlist[errno]);
    else
        printf("unknown error\n");
    exit(1);
}
```

The anticipated error situation may now be simply handled as follows:

```
if (sysinfo(SI_SET_HOSTNAME, buffer, strlen(buffer)+1) == -1)
    report_err("set hostname");
```

The library function `perror()` implements a similar functionality, and thus, `report_err()` merely serves as an illustration.

6. 4   Summary

The following points were discussed in this short introductory chapter:

§   The UNIX operating system validates system calls to preserve its integrity.

§   From a C program, a system call has the same syntax as a function call.

§   The documentation of system calls and library routines are found in sections 2 and 3 of standard UNIX manuals. The description for each system call includes the parameters that will accompany the routine, and the interpretion of the results obtained.

§   The results of system calls must be checked for error conditions so that contingency plans can be taken.

In subsequent chapters, system and library calls pertaining to file manipulation, process creation, signals and terminal handling will be reviewed. The material presented in these chapters merely give a quick overview of the facilities available. Their general usage is illustrated with sample code fragments. Readers should still refer to the respective manual pages for comprehensive treatment of each individual call.

The `intro(2)` man page provides a comprehensive overview of error conditions and UNIX terminology. A similar overview may also be found in the SunOS 5.x System Services Manual.

7

File Manipulation

The methods for reading from a file, pipe or character device, or writing to them, share a common characteristic. These operations are performed via the *file descriptor* that is returned when the file, pipe or device is initially opened. The UNIX file system consists of many files that a user can potentially access. However, a file descriptor represents the dynamic state of operating on a file. Thus, two or more programs may read the same file without interference since the state of reading the same file is represented by a different file descriptor (in each program).

A file descriptor is an integer index into the file descriptor table. Each UNIX process is provided with a typical figure of between twenty to sixty-four file descriptors. Since a file description represents how a file is being manipulated by a program, this number is the maximum number of files that may be manipulated by a program at any single time. Of this total number, the first three are by convention opened with standard meanings. File descriptor 0 is the standard input and file descriptor 1 is the standard output. These provide a program with the standard means of reading and writing. These descriptors are normally bound to the keyboard and display screen respectively. Thus, reading from the keyboard or writing to the screen need not be preceded by any open calls.

File descriptor 2 is the standard error stream. As the name suggests, it is usually reserved for error or warning messages. It is also typically bound to the display screen. In this instance, it is useful to bind different descriptors to the same screen device because they represent different functionalities: one for error reporting, and the other for output typically expected from a program. The rationale for and benefits derived from this will be clearer when mechanisms for input/output redirection are examined later on.

The first three file descriptors are also known as STDIN_FILENO, STDOUT_FILENO and STDERR_FILENO.

In the light of this strategy of separating error messages and normal output, the function report_err() would be better coded as follows:

```
void report_err(char *prefix)
{
    extern int errno;
    extern int sys_nerr;
    extern char *sys_errlist[];

    if (prefix != NULL)
        fprintf(stderr, "%s: ", prefix);
    if (0 < errno && errno < sys_nerr)
        fprintf(stderr, "%s\n", sys_errlist[errno]);
    else
        fprintf(stderr, "unknown error code\n");
    exit(1);
}
```

Here, stderr is the file pointer associated with the standard error stream, and fprintf() is the equivalent of printf() which allows a file pointer to be specified. Operations involving file pointers (as opposed to file descriptors) will be discussed later in this chapter.

7. 1   Reading and Writing Files

The facilities for reading and writing files are provided by the creat(), open(), read(), write() and close() system calls. If the creat() and open() calls succeed in opening a file, they return appropriate file descriptors for writing or reading or both, depending on supplied options. The close() system call performs the complementary function of open(). It indicates that a file descriptor is no longer required, and might thus be recycled for use in a subsequent open operation. Finally, as the names suggest, the read() and write() calls perform appropriate read and write operations on the specified file descriptor.

a. **creat()** **system call** – creates a new file or rewrite an existing one

```
#include <sys/types.h>
#include <sys/stat.h>
#include <fcntl.h>

int creat(char *path, mode_t mode);
```

If the file named by path does not already exist, creat() creates and opens it for writing if the parent directory is writable. The file ownership is set to the user of the process making the call, and file-access permissions are set as in mode.

If the file already exists and is writable, its length is truncated to 0 before it is opened for writing. In this case, the permissions as in mode are ignored, and the ownership and access permissions of the file remain unchanged.

File-access permissions are those shown in a long directory listing:

```
$ ls -l .profile
-rw-r--r--    1 dkiong    compsc        719 Nov  8  1993  .profile
```

While symbolic names such as rwx are used to represent file permissions in UNIX command utilities like ls or chmod, they are represented by an integer in the actual file system. A suitable three-digit octal is formed by a bitwise OR | operation on the symbolic constants as defined in /usr/include/sys/stat.h and reproduced in Table 7-1.

Symbol	Value	Remarks
S_IRWXU	0700	read, write, execute by owner
S_IRUSR	0400	read permission by owner
S_IWUSR	0200	write permission by owner
S_IXUSR	0100	execute permission by owner
S_IRWXG	0070	read, write, execute by group members
S_IRGRP	0040	read permission by group members
S_IWGRP	0020	write permission by group members
S_IXGRP	0010	execute permission by group members
S_IRWXO	0007	read, write, execute by others
S_IROTH	0004	read permission by others
S_IWOTH	0002	write permission by others
S_IXOTH	0001	execute permission by others

Table 7-1: Permission mode values

Upon successful completion, creat() returns a (lowest integer) file descriptor for writing.

The octal number 0640 is used to create a file which is readable and writable to self, read-only to group members, and not accessible to others. This is often easier using the symbolic constants above, as illustrated in the following code fragment:

```
int fd;

fd = creat(".project", S_IRUSR|S_IWUSR|S_IRGRP);
```

A write request may then be attempted on an opened file descriptor.

b. `write()` system call – writes to a file

```
#include <unistd.h>

ssize_t write(int fildes, void *buf, size_t nbyte);
```

The `write()` system call attempts to write `nbyte` bytes from the buffer address `buf` to the file descriptor specified by `fildes`. On completion, it returns the number of bytes that was written. Normally, it would be the same as `nbyte`.

For non-blocking[1] write operations, the number of bytes written could be less than `nbyte`. This is not considered an error, and the write operation should be repeated, though without the buffer prefix that has already been written.

As with other calls, a return value of -1 indicates an error situation, the nature of which is revealed through `errno`.

When operations to a file are completed, a `close()` system call reclaims the storage required to represent the state of a file.

c. `close()` system call – closes a file descriptor

```
#include <unistd.h>

int close(int fildes);
```

`close()` closes the file descriptor indicated by `fildes`. Closing a file descriptor makes it available for use by another `open()` or `creat()` operation. On completion, `close()` returns 0 to indicate success, but -1 if `fildes` was not a valid opened file descriptor.

---

[1] Non-blocking write operations are briefly discussed in chapter 11.

d. echoTo sample program

The creat(), write() and close() system calls may be used to implement a trivial echoTo program as shown in Listing 7-1. It uses the first argument as the destination file and writes subsequent arguments into it.

```
#include <unistd.h>
#include <sys/stat.h>

main(int argc, char *argv[])
{
    int i, fd;

    if (argc == 1)   /* no arguments */
        exit(0);      /* just exit */
    fd = creat(argv[1], S_IRUSR|S_IWUSR|S_IRGRP|S_IROTH);
    if (fd == -1)
        report_err(argv[1]);
    for (i = 2; i<argc; i++)
        if (write(fd, argv[i], strlen(argv[i])) != strlen(argv[i]) ||
            write(fd, "\n", 1) != 1)
          report_err(argv[1]);
    if (close(fd) == -1)
      report_err(argv[1]);
    exit(0);
}
```

Listing 7-1: echoTo program

While the program fulfills its objective, note that UNIX utilities generally do not use command-line arguments for destination files, nor do they prompt for their names. The former increases the likelihood of accidentally overwriting an existing file. The latter restricts its usage with pipes[2]. Output to a file is typically achieved by redirecting the standard output[3] when invoking the command from the shell.

---

[2] Pipes are discussed in the next chapter.

[3] Input and output redirection are also discussed in the next chapter.

e. `open()` system call – opens file for reading or writing

```
#include <sys/types.h>
#include <sys/stat.h>
#include <fcntl.h>

int open(char *path, int oflag [, mode_t mode ]);
```

The `open()` system call opens a file named `path` with the set of operation flags `oflag`, and file permissions `mode` as in the case of `creat()`. Operation flags are constructed by bitwise OR | operations of the symbolic constants in Table 7-2.

Symbol	Remarks
O_RDONLY	Open file for reading only.
O_WRONLY	Open file for writing only.
O_RDWR	Open file for both reading and writing.

Table 7-2: Mandatory operation flags

One of the operation flags O_RDONLY, O_WRONLY or O_RDWR must be included in the `oflag` mask for the `open()` system call. The flags in Table 7-3 elaborate on how files are created and written to.

Symbol	Remarks
O_APPEND	By default, reading and writing start at the beginning of the file. In the case of writing to an existing file, this implies overwriting the initial portions of a file. If O_APPEND is set, write operations will always occur at the end of the file.
O_CREAT	By default, a file must exist before it can be opened for writing via `open()`. If O_CREAT is set, `open()` will create the file if it does not already exist. This flag has no effect if the file already exists, except when O_EXCL (below) is also set.

Symbol	Remarks
O_EXCL	If O_EXCL and O_CREAT are set, open() will fail if the file already exists. Note that the check for the existence of the file and creation of the file is atomic[4]. Integrity will not be compromised by interaction with another process having the same request.
O_TRUNC	By default, writing to an existing file either overwrites the initial file contents or is appended to the end of the file. If O_TRUNC is set, the length of an existing file is truncated to 0 and the mode and owner left unchanged.

Table 7-3: Optional operation flags

In fact, with the attributes above, the creat() system call is no longer required, but exists only for historic and compatibility reasons. It is unnecessary since creat(path,mode) is equivalent to open(path,O_WRONLY|O_CREAT|O_TRUNC,mode).

~ p95/96 for modes

As with creat(), upon successful completion, open() returns a (lowest number) file descriptor for either reading, writing or both (depending on oflag).

f. read() system call – reads from a file

```
#include <sys/types.h>
#include <sys/uio.h>
#include <unistd.h>

ssize_t read(int fildes, void *buf, size_t nbyte);
```

read() attempts to read nbyte bytes from the file associated with fildes into the buffer address buf.

When completed, read() returns the number of bytes that has been read. Typically, it would be the same as nbyte unless the end of the file has been encountered, or data is not yet available when reading in non-blocking mode.

Like other calls, a return value of -1 indicates an error situation, the nature of which is revealed through errno.

---

[4] Being an atomic action, the UNIX system kernel ensures that the file will not be created by another process between the periods of checking for the presence of the file and creating it.

7.2   Non-sequence File Access

Since a file descriptor represents the dynamic state of manipulating a file, it maintains a count of what has been written or read. This file position is in terms of a count of bytes from the beginning of the file, a 0 offset indicating the start of a file.

When a file is opened, the file position is by default placed at the beginning of the file. However, the O_APPEND option causes file pointer to be set at the end of the file.

Since file access in UNIX is sequential, read and write operations start at the file position associated with the file descriptor. In effect, such operations cause the file position to be incremented by the number of bytes read or written.

The lseek() system call explicitly repositions the file position within a file so that access need not be sequential.

a. lseek() system call – changes the read/write file pointer position

```
#include <sys/types.h>
#include <unistd.h>

off_t lseek(int fildes, off_t offset, int whence);
```

The lseek() system call sets the file position for the next read or write operation associated with the opened file descriptor fildes. The interpretation of the new position offset depends on the three possible values of whence, as enumerated in Table 7-4.

whence	New file position
SEEK_SET	file position is set to offset bytes
SEEK_CUR	file position is set to its current location plus offset
SEEK_END	file position is set to the size of the file minus offset

Table 7-4: whence position options in lseek()

The options for whence allow repositioning of the file position according to

- an absolute position,

- a relative position (from the current offset) or

- a position from the end of the file.

On success, the lseek() system call returns the resulting file pointer location, as measured in bytes from the beginning of the file. Note that off_t is defined as long int.

7.3 Directory Operations

The system calls for creating, writing and reading files have been discussed, and we now turn to directory operations. The following system calls allow for the creation and deletion of directories, deletion of directory entries and query for a directory listing.

A directory may be created and removed using the system calls mkdir() and rmdir() respectively. The UNIX commands mkdir and rmdir happen to have the same name as the system call. However, it should be clear that this is merely a coincidence and these commands are implemented using the corresponding system calls.

a. mkdir() system call – creates a directory

```
#include <sys/types.h>
#include <sys/stat.h>

int mkdir(char *path, mode_t mode);
```

The mkdir() system call creates a new directory named path. The mode of the new directory is initialised from mode, and similar with that used for creat(). Note that for a file to be accessible, all directories leading to it must be at least searchable (i.e. have executable permissions).

b. rmdir() system call – removes a directory

```
#include <unistd.h>

int rmdir(char *path);
```

The rmdir() system call removes the directory named path. A directory to be removed must be empty, and only contain entries for " . " and " .. ".

c. `unlink()` system call – removes directory entry

```
#include <unistd.h>

int unlink(char *path);
```

The `unlink()` system call removes the directory entry named by `path` and decrements the link count of the file referenced by the directory entry. (File links are discussed in the next section.)

Note that adding a directory entry is already implied by the `creat()` and `open()` system calls to create new files.

A directory listing may be obtained using the `opendir()`, `readdir()` and `closedir()` routines. The method is analogous to reading a normal file via the `open()`, `read()` and `close()` system calls.

d. `opendir()`, `readdir()` and `closedir()` library calls – list directory entries

```
#include <dirent.h>

DIR *opendir(char *dirname);
struct dirent *readdir(DIR *dirp);
int closedir(DIR *dirp);
```

The `opendir()` library routine opens a directory named `dirname`, and returns a directory stream. A NULL directory stream indicates that `dirname` is not a valid directory.

Subsequently, each call to `readdir()` reads a directory entry from the specified directory stream. It returns the information in a `struct dirent` data structure. This representation is independent of the file system type chosen by the system administrator.

A NULL result from `readdir()` indicates the end of the directory stream. Following this condition, `closedir()` is invoked to deallocate associated data structures.

Since directories are special catalogue files, Table 7-5 summarises the analogous relationship between file and directory operations.

File	Directory
File is opened with `open()` system call.	Directory is opened with `opendir()` library call.
`open()` returns a stream to read in the form of an integer file descriptor.	`opendir()` returns a directory stream to read in the form of a pointer to DIR.

File	Directory
read() returns char sequence from file.	readdir() returns struct dirent to represent an entry from directory.
close() allows file descriptor to be reused.	closedir() allows data structures to be deallocated.

Table 7-5: Similarities between reading a file and a directory

The code in Listing 7-2 illustrates a simple directory-listing program. In addition to the name of each directory entry, it also includes the *inode* number.

```c
#include <stdio.h>
#include <dirent.h>

main(int argc, char *argv[])
{
  char *name;
  DIR *dirp;
  struct dirent *direntp;

  if (argc > 1)
    name = argv[1];
  else
    name = ".";
  dirp = opendir(name);
  if (dirp == NULL)
    report_err(name);
  direntp = readdir(dirp);
  while (direntp != NULL) {
    printf("%s\n", direntp->d_name);
    direntp = readdir(dirp);
  }
  if (closedir(dirp) == -1)
    report_err(name);
  exit(0);
}
```

Listing 7-2: Directory listing

7. 4   File Links

So far, we have seen a directory as a file catalogue. A directory is created via the mkdir() system call, and deleted via rmdir(). A directory entry is added when a new file is created, as seen previously via creat(), or open() with O_WRONLY and O_CREAT flags. The complementary action occurs when a file is deleted via unlink().

To gain a better understanding of the UNIX file system, writing a new file actually involves three modifications to the file system representation:

- A list of disk blocks is allocated to store the contents of the file proper.

- An *inode* block is allocated to contain file information such as attributes like its owner, time of creation, file size, access permissions, and most importantly, the disk block locations of where the contents of the file are physically stored.

- An entry in the parent directory with an *inode* reference. This ultimately maps a pathname to its *inode* block.

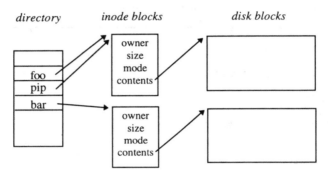

Figure 7-1: File organisation

The UNIX file system strategy of representing directory entries by links to *inode* blocks allows a file to be accessed via more than one pathname. This merely involves linking another directory entry (corresponding to a new pathname) to an existing *inode* block. File-link creation thus modifies the parent directory, but does not require additional *inodes*.

It follows that file deletion involves severing the link to the *inode* and deleting the corresponding directory entry. Furthermore, the *inode* block and corresponding disk blocks containing the file contents may be reclaimed, if there are no more links to it and no process has opened the file.

a. link() system call – creates a link to a file

```
#include <unistd.h>

int link(char *existing, char *new);
```

The link() system call creates a new directory entry by inserting a link to the *inode* entry of an existing file. existing is the name of an existing file. new is the name of the new directory entry to be added.

The *inode* block contains a count of the number of links to a file. link() thus increments this count by one.

7.5   File Attributes

Each file is associated with attributes, e.g. the size of file, time of last modification, owner of the file, and access permissions. Given a pathname or an opened file descriptor, the stat() and fstat() system calls return file-status information via an instance of struct stat. While some file attributes are set implicitly through creating and modifying the file, the chmod() and chown() system calls are used to modify file-access permissions and ownership respectively.

a. stat() and fstat() system calls – get file status

```
#include <sys/types.h>
#include <sys/stat.h>

int stat(char *path, struct stat *buf);

int fstat(int fildes, struct stat *buf);
```

The stat() system call obtains information about the file pointed to by path. Read, write, or execute permissions of the named file is not required. However, all directories listed in the pathname leading to the file must be searchable (a directory is searchable if its mode is executable). stat() returns 0 to indicate success, and –1 otherwise.

The fstat() system call obtains information about an opened file via the file descriptor fildes. fildes might be obtained from a successful open(), creat(), dup() or pipe()[5] call.

buf is the address of a stat structure into which information is placed concerning the file. A struct stat instance contains the information as summarised in Table 7-6 (the table is not comprehensive):

---

[5] dup() and pipe() are discussed in the next chapter.

struct stat field	Usage
mode_t st_mode;	File type and mode
nlink_t st_nlink;	Number of links
uid_t st_uid;	User ID of the file's owner
gid_t st_gid;	Group ID of the file's group
off_t st_size;	File size in bytes
time_t st_atime;	Time of last access
time_t st_mtime;	Time of last data modification
time_t st_ctime;	Time of last file-status change

Table 7-6: File stat *information*

The type mode_t is sufficiently large to hold both the type and access mode of the file. The lower bits of st_mode hold the file-access permissions and are the same as those for creat() and open(). The upper bits contain file-type information such as whether the file is a regular file or a directory. These instances may be queried via S_ISREG() and S_ISDIR() respectively. Codes are available for other devices and are discussed in greater detail in stat(2) man pages.

Each user in the system has a login name. Often, this identifier is more for the convenience of users. The ls and ps utilities display such names to indicate the owners of files and processes respectively. However, the UNIX operating system records process and file ownership via an integer ID. The user ID and group ID are integers chosen by the system administrator for this purpose. The mapping between login name and user ID is specified in the password file. The information in the password file will be discussed in chapter 9.

Time is measured in seconds since 00:00:00 UTC, January 1, 1970. Time representations and appropriate conversion functions will also be discussed in chapter 9.

b. chmod() and fchmod() system calls – change the access permission of file

```
#include <sys/types.h>
#include <sys/stat.h>

int chmod(char *path, mode_t mode);
int fchmod(int fildes, mode_t mode);
```

The chmod() system call sets the file-access permission of the file named path to the bit pattern contained in mode. The fchmod() system call serves the same functionality, but instead refers to the opened file descriptor fildes.

c. chown() and fchown() system calls – change the owner and group of a file

```
#include <unistd.h>
#include <sys/types.h>

int chown(char *path, uid_t owner, gid_t group);

int fchown(int fildes, uid_t owner, gid_t group);
```

The chown() system call sets the owner ID and group ID of the file named path to owner and group respectively. If owner or group is specified as -1, chown() will not change the corresponding ID of the file. The fchown() system call serves the same functions, but refers to the opened file descriptor fildes.

7. 6   Buffering Input/Output Operations

The read() and write() system calls provide a simple yet flexible means of reading and writing varying amounts of data. A limited amount of kernel-level buffering is performed so that data movements coincide with disk block size. However, the calls are particularly expensive for reading and writing small quantities of data.

A simple file-copying function, like the one provided below, will confirm this.

```
char buf[BUFFERSIZE];

void copy(char *source, char *dest)
{
    int n, src, dst;

    if ((src = open(source, O_RDONLY)) == -1)
      report_err(source);
    if ((dst = open(dest, O_WRONLY|O_CREAT|O_TRUNC)) == -1)
      report_err(dest);
    while ((n = read(src, buf, BUFFERSIZE)) > 0)
       write(dst, buf, n);

    if (close(src) == -1)
      report_err(source);
    if (close(dst) == -1)
      report_err(dest);
}
```

By including the necessary header files and an appropriate main() function, the program is compiled twice with BUFFERSIZE values of 8 and 512. The timing results in Table 7-7 were obtained from copying a 1MB data file. It shows that the `read()` and `write()` system calls favour larger transfer units during input/output operations.

	real time	user time	system time
copy with BUFFERSIZE=8	28.2	3.7	24.9
copy with BUFFERSIZE=512	1.9	0.1	0.8

Table 7-7: Writing with different buffer sizes

The *stdio* library package was designed to overcome this efficiency problem by providing user-level buffering. It works by redirecting *stdio* calls to write to a file into the associated buffer. When it is filled, a `write()` system call will physical flush the contents of the buffer. Similarly, a `read()` system call prereads file contents into a sufficiently large buffer. *stdio* calls to read from a file are then serviced from this buffer.

In addition to buffering, the *stdio* library package also provides functions for a varied repertoire of data types, ranging from character, word to string. The formatted input/output feature allows for the format of output and input to be conveniently specified.

7.7 *stdio* Library Package

The *stdio* library package implements a higher level abstraction called streams. A stream corresponds to a file descriptor when using the `read()` and `write()` system calls directly. It is represented by a pointer to a FILE structure.

A file is opened by calling the `fopen()` library routine. If the operation is successful, a FILE pointer is returned, just as `open()` returns a file descriptor for subsequent I/O operations. Similarly, the `fclose()` routine closes the stream. Again, this is analogous to the `close()` system call which allows a file descriptor to be reused.

While the FILE structure provides the appropriate data structures and necessary buffer mechanism, *stdio* routines must ultimately still rely on a corresponding file descriptor. The implementation of the `fopen()` and `fclose()` routines must be implemented by the `open()` and `close()` system calls. Similarly, buffered read and write operations must be implemented by the `read()` and `write()` system calls respectively.

The predefined file pointers stdin, stdout and stderr correspond to the standard STDIN_FILENO, STDOUT_FILENO and STDERR_FILENO file descriptors.

a. `fopen()` and `fdopen()` library routines – open a stream

```
#include <stdio.h>

FILE *fopen(char *filename, char *mode);
FILE *fdopen(int fildes, char *mode);
```

The `fopen()` routine opens the file `filename` and returns a FILE pointer associated with the stream. `mode` determines how the file is to be manipulated. It is one of the character strings enumerated in Table 7-8.

On the other hand, the `fdopen()` routine uses the file represented by the opened file descriptor `fildes` and returns a FILE pointer associated with it. The operation mode of `fildes` must correspond with the supplied `mode`. In both cases, a NULL result indicates that the operation was unsuccessful.

Mode	Remarks
`"r"`	open `filename` for reading
`"w"`	open `filename` for writing. (If the file does not exist, it is first created. If the file already exists, its length is truncated to zero.)
`"a"`	open `filename` for writing. (If the file does not exist, it is first created. If the file already exists, the file pointer is always set to the end before writing.)
`"r+"`	open `filename` for update (reading and writing).
`"w+"`	open `filename` for update (reading and writing). (If the file does not exist, it is first created. If the file already exists, its length is truncated to zero.)
`"a+"`	open `filename` for update (reading and writing). (If the file does not exist, it is first created. If the file already exists, the file pointer is always set to the end before writing.)

Table 7-8: File opening modes for streams

b. `fclose()` library routine – closes a stream

```
#include <stdio.h>

int fclose(FILE *s);
```

The `fclose()` routine closes the stream `s`. Any buffered data waiting to be written will be flushed out. `fclose()` is also performed automatically for all opened files upon calling `exit()`.

   `fclose()` returns 0 to indicate successful completion of the operation. Otherwise, an error condition is indicated by EOF.

c. `fflush()` library routine – flushes a stream

```
#include <stdio.h>

int fflush(FILE *stream);
```

For an output or update stream to which the most recent operation was not input, `fflush()` writes buffered data in `stream` to the associated file. Any unread data buffered in `stream` is discarded.

   If `stream` is a NULL pointer, `fflush()` flushes all files opened for writing.

d. *stdio* output functions

The output functions via streams are summarised in this section. They generally return the number of bytes written out. The formatted specifications for the output function `printf()` and its variants are more complex, and are elaborated on in the next section.

`int putc(int c, FILE *stream);`	`putc()` writes `c` (converted to an unsigned char) to `stream`
`int putchar(int c);`	`putchar(c)` is defined as `putc(c, stdout)`
`int fputc(int c, FILE *stream);`	`fputc()` behaves like `putc()`, but is a function rather than a macro.
`int putw(int w, FILE *stream);`	`putw()` writes an integer `w` to `stream`

```
int puts(char *s);
```

puts() writes the null-terminated string pointed to by s, followed by a newline character, to stdout

```
int fputs(char *s, FILE *stream);
```

fputs() writes the null-terminated string pointed to by s to stream

```
size_t fwrite
    (void *ptr, size_t size,
    size_t nitems, FILE *stream);
```

fwrite() writes the nitems data items of size size pointed to by ptr to stream

```
int printf
    (char *format [, arg...]);
```

formatted print to stdout

```
int fprintf(FILE *stream,
            char *format [,arg...]);
```

formatted print to stream

```
int *sprintf
    (char *s, char *format [,arg...]);
```

formatted print to string buffer s

e. `printf()` and formatted output specifications

The formatted output routines printf() and fprintf() work according to the format specification and corresponding argument values. format is a character string which contains two types of objects: plain characters and conversion specifications. Plain characters are simply copied to the output stream. Conversion specifications specify the output form of the arguments args.

The routine sprintf() works in a similar fashion, except that the resultant string is not output into a stream, but buffered in the character string buf. Note that the buffer buf must be pre-allocated and sufficiently large to hold the formatted result.

The correspondence between conversion specifications and arguments args imply that the result is undefined if there are insufficient arguments for the format. If however, the format is exhausted while arguments remain, the excess arguments are simply ignored.

Each conversion specification is distinguished by a **%** character and has the general form:

% {flag} [field_width] [. precision] [**l**] type

The mandatory conversion type characters and corresponding meaning are as follows:

d,i,o, The integer arg is converted to signed decimal (d or i), unsigned octal (o), unsigned
u,x,X   decimal (u), or unsigned hexadecimal notation (x and X), respectively. The letters
        abcdef are used for x conversion and the letters ABCDEF for X conversion.

f   The float or double `arg` is converted to decimal notation in the style `"[-]ddd.ddd"`. The number of digits after the decimal point is equal to the precision specification. If the `precision` is missing, six digits are given.

e,E   The float or double `arg` is converted in the style `"[-]d.ddde_ddd"`. There is one digit before the decimal point and the number of digits after it is equal to the `precision`. If the `precision` is missing, six digits are produced. The E format code will produce a number with E instead of e introducing the exponent.

g,G   The float or double `arg` is printed in style f or e (or in style E in the case of a G format code). The style used depends on the value converted: style e or E will be used only if the exponent resulting from the conversion is less than -4 or greater than the `precision`. Trailing zeroes are removed from the result; a decimal point appears only if it is followed by a digit.

c   The character `arg` is printed.

s   The `arg` is taken to be a character pointer and characters from the string are printed until a null character is encountered or until the number of characters indicated by the `precision` specification is reached. If the `precision` is missing, it is taken to be infinite, so all characters up to the first null character are printed.

%   No argument is converted; print a %.

The `flag` characters and their meanings are as follows:

–   The result of the conversion will be left-justified within the field.

+   The result of a signed conversion will always begin with a sign (+ or -).

blank   If the first character of a signed conversion is not a sign, a blank will be prefixed to the result. This implies that if the blank and + flags both appear, the blank flag will be ignored.

This flag specifies that the value is to be converted to an alternate form. For c, d, i, s, and u conversions, the flag has no effect. For o conversion, it increases the `precision` to force the first digit of the result to be a zero. For x or X conversion, a non-zero result will have 0x or 0X prefixed to it. For e, E, f, g, and G conversions, the result will always contain a decimal point, even if no digits follow the point (normally, a decimal point appears in the result of these conversions only if a digit follows it). For g and G conversions, trailing zeroes will not be removed from the result (which they normally are).

•   `field width` is an optional decimal digit string such that if the converted value has fewer characters than specified, it will be padded on the left (or right, if the left-adjustment flag '-' has been given). The padding is with blanks unless the `field width` digit string starts with a zero, in which case the padding is with zeros.

- precision gives the minimum number of digits to appear for the d, i, o, u, x, or X conversions, the number of digits to appear after the decimal point for the e, E, and f conversions, the maximum number of significant digits for the g and G conversion, or the maximum number of characters to be printed from a string in s conversion. Padding specified by the precision overrides the padding specified by the field width.

- An optional l specifies that a following d, i, o, u, x, or X conversion character applies to a long integer arg. An l before any other conversion character is ignored.

- field width and precision may be indicated by an asterisk '*' instead of a digit string. In such a case, an integer arg supplies the field width or precision. The argument that is actually converted is not fetched until the conversion letter is seen, so the arguments specifying field width or precision must appear before the argument to be converted. A negative field width argument is taken as a '-' flag followed by a positive field width.

Upon successful completion, printf(), fprintf() and sprintf() return the number of characters transmitted, excluding the null character.

f. *stdio* input functions

The input functions via streams are summarised in this section. In most cases, these input functions are the complements of the output functions above.

```
int getc(FILE *stream);
```
getc() returns the next character (that is, byte) from stream

```
int getchar(void);
```
getchar() is defined as getc(stdin)

```
int fgetc(FILE *stream);
```
fgetc() behaves like getc(), but is a function rather than a macro

```
int getw(FILE *stream);
```
getw() returns the next word (that is, integer) from stream

```
char *gets(char *s);
```
gets() reads characters from stdin into the array pointed to by s, until a newline character is read or an end-of-file condition is encountered

```
char *fgets
      (char *s, int n, FILE *stream);
```
fgets() reads characters from stream into the buffer pointed to by s, until n-1 characters are read, or a newline character or an end-of-file condition is encountered

```
size_t fread(void *ptr, size_t size,
      size_t nitems, FILE *stream);
```
fread() reads from stream into the buffer pointed to by ptr up to nitems data items of size size

```
int scanf(char *format [,pointer...]);          formatted read from stdin

int fscanf(FILE *stream, char *format           formatted read from stream
          [,pointer...]);

int sscanf(char *inp, char *format              formatted read from string buffer inp
          [,pointer...]);
```

g. scanf() and formatted input specifications

The formatted input routines scanf() and fscanf() read according to control specifications in format. The result is stored in variables referenced by corresponding pointer arguments. The control string contains three types of objects:

- white-space characters (such as SPACE, TAB and NEWLINE) which cause input to be read up to the next non-white-space character,

- ordinary characters (apart from '%') which must match the next character of the input stream, and

- conversion specifications which direct the interpretation of input sequences and store the results in the variables referenced by the corresponding argument.

The result is undefined if there are insufficient arguments for the format. If the format is exhausted while arguments remain, the excess pointers are simply ignored.

The sscanf() routine works in a similar fashion except that input is obtained from the string inp.

Each conversion specification is distinguished by a **%** character and has the general form:

```
% [*] [width] [l|h] type
```

The mandatory conversion type characters and their corresponding meanings are as follows:

%	A single % is expected in the input at this point; no assignment is performed.
d,o,x	A decimal (d), octal (o) or hexadecimal (x) integer is expected; the corresponding argument should be an integer pointer.
u	An unsigned decimal integer is expected; the corresponding argument should be an unsigned integer pointer.
i	An integer is expected and interpreted according to C conventions: a leading '0' implies octal; a leading '0x' implies hexadecimal, otherwise, it is decimal; the corresponding argument should be an integer pointer.

f   A floating-point number is expected; the next field is converted accordingly
          and stored through the corresponding argument, which should be a float pointer.

s   A character string is expected; the corresponding argument should be a
          character pointer to a block large enough to accept the string.

c   A character is expected; the corresponding argument should be a character
          pointer. The normal skip over white-spaces is suppressed in this case; to read
          the next non-space character, use %1s.

[scanset] The input field is the maximal sequence of input characters consisting entirely
           of characters in the scanset. The circumflex ^, when it appears as the first
           character in the scanset, serves as a complement operator and redefines the
           scanset as the set of all characters not contained in the remainder of the
           scanset string.

- The suppression of assignment as indicated by '*' provides a way of describing an input
  field which is to be skipped.

- The optional width specifies the maximum length of the input field.

- The conversion characters d, u, o, x, and i may be preceded by l or h to indicate a pointer
  to long or to short, rather than to int in the argument list. Similarly, the conversion
  character f may be preceded by l to indicate a pointer to double rather than to float in
  the argument list.

scanf() conversion terminates at the end of file (EOF), at the end of the control string, or when
an input character conflicts with the control string. In the last case, the offending character is
left unread in the input stream.

    scanf() returns the number of successfully matched and assigned input items; this
number can be zero in the event of an early conflict between an input character and the control
string. The constant EOF is returned upon end of input.

h. Adjusting the file position with the **fseek()** library routine

As a result of the buffering performed by the *stdio* package, it requires auxillary routines for
explicitly moving the file position. Just as the lseek() system call moves the file position of
the associated file descriptor, the fseek() library routine provides for the same functionality
for streams.

```
#include <stdio.h>

int fseek(FILE *stream, long offset, int placement);

long ftell(FILE *stream);
```

The `fseek()` library routine sets the position of the next input or output operation on `stream`. This new position is at `offset` bytes from the beginning, the current position, or the end of the file, as indicated by `placement` values: SEEK_SET, SEEK_CUR, or SEEK_END. Note that these symbols are the same as those used with the `lseek()` system call (see Table 7-4) and that the parameter serves the same purpose as `whence` there.

`fseek()` returns 0 to indicate a successful repositioning, and –1 to indicate an erroneous situation.

The `ftell()` library routine performs the complementary role of `fseek()` by indicating the current file position relative to the beginning of the file in question.

7. 8   Mixing *stdio* Operations with System Calls

The *stdio* library is advantageous because it provides

- user-level buffering, and

- a wide range of input/output operations for different data formats.

The latter is evident by comparing allowable arguments and formats for the `printf()` and `scanf()` library routines with those for the `write()` and `read()` system calls.

The relationship between application programs, the *stdio* library and system calls is illustrated in Figure 7-2.

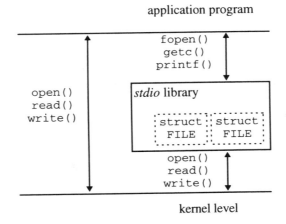

Figure 7-2: Relationship between system calls and the stdio library

The buffers maintained by FILE structures imply that usage of the two levels of read and write operators can only be mixed with care. Consider the output produced by the program in Listing 7-3.

```
#include <unistd.h>
#include <stdio.h>

void main()
{
    char *mesg1 = "This is written via printf()";
    char *mesg2 = "This is written via write()";

    printf("%s", mesg1);
    write(STDOUT_FILENO, mesg2, strlen(mesg2));
    exit(0);
}
```

Listing 7-3: Mixing buffered and unbuffered operations

The two messages appear in different orders because the message printed by printf() remains in the buffer until flushed out by exit(). The fflush() routine is used in Listing 7-4 to maintain a correct output sequence.

```
#include <unistd.h>
#include <stdio.h>

void main()
{
    char *mesg1 = "This is written via printf()";
    char *mesg2 = "This is written via write()";

    printf("%s", mesg1);
    fflush(stdout);
    write(STDOUT_FILENO, mesg2, strlen(mesg2));
    exit(0);
}
```

Listing 7-4: Flushing a bufferred stream

7. 9 Summary

This chapter has introduced the UNIX system calls for basic file manipulation via file descriptors and directory operations. Useful library calls from *stdio* have also been included. These may be classified as follows:

§   Open and close files

    `open(), creat(), close()`

§   Read and write operations

    `read(), write()`

§   File pointer repositioning

    `lseek()`

§   Directory and link operations

    `mkdir(), rmdir(), unlink(), link()`

§   Directory listing

    `opendir(), readdir(), closedir()`

§   File ownership and access permissions

    `chmod(), fchmod(), chown(), fchown()`

§   *stdio* routines

```
fopen(), fclose(), fflush()
putc(), putchar(), fputc(), putw(), puts(), fputs(), fwrite(),
    printf(), fprintf(), sprintf()
getc(), getchar(), fgetc(), getw(), gets(), fgets(), fread(),
    scanf(), fscanf(), sscanf()
fseek(), ftell()
```

7. 10   Exercises

1.   Allow the browser to read the contents of standard input rather than a file.

2.   Extend the browser to allow for multibuffer and multiwindow capabilities. Note that this feature is useful for the editor too.

3.   Extend command-line processing so that when multiple file names occur in the command line, they will be read into multiple buffers.

8

UNIX Processes

The UNIX operating system manages disk devices to provide a virtual file system for each user. In the previous chapter, we discussed the various operations on the UNIX file system. We now study the process environment in which a compiled C program is executed.

It would seem as though a multi-user machine is capable of simultaneously executing many independent tasks. In reality, a CPU is assigned to each task for a fraction of the time. When a task has been executed long enough and consumed its time allocation (or time slice), the operating system withdraws the CPU resource from it. In turn, the CPU is assigned to the next task which has been waiting to continue. The scheduling and context switching occurs fast enough such that it seems as though all tasks are being executed simultaneously.

When a CPU is withdrawn from a task, the UNIX kernel must save sufficient context information. This might include the CPU registers and flags. When a CPU is eventually reassigned to a task, the kernel must restore the context which was previously saved. This allows execution to resume as though the discontinuation never occurred. The UNIX kernel may thus be seen as providing a virtual CPU for each task. Each unit task is called a process in the UNIX operating system.

The address space of a UNIX process does not overlap with that of another. If this was not so, a process may interfere with another by altering (intentionally or unintentionally) its data and thus producing non-deterministic results. Hence, each process executes code independent of other processes.

8. 1   The Process Environment

It is useful to consider the basic environment in which programs are executed: A program is typically specified from the command line. The interactive shell parses the command line to obtain the program name in question and associated program parameters. This is the standard means of supplying program parameters. Program flexibility is enhanced since its behaviour is fine-tuned when execution begins.

After the shell spawns a new process, its code is immediately overlaid with the code of the program to be executed. Parameters are stored in a suitable representation so that a program ultimately accesses them via the argc and argv parameters.

A process also has access to a list of environment variables. For example, at login time, the login script sets the environment variable MAIL to the location of the user's mailbox. These variables are also implicitly inherited, and provide another means by which customisation of programs could be performed as late as possible.

It should be clear that shell variables comprise both local and exported variables. The former may be represented internally via a table or dictionary mechanism. Given a variable, the shell can determine its corresponding value by looking up the table. Exported variables share the usage patterns with local variables. Since they are inherited by child processes, they rely on environment variables.

The program in Listing 8-1 shows how program arguments and environment variables are accessed. envp is typically not included since it has the same value as environ.

```
extern char **environ;

main(int argc, char *argv[], char **envp)
{
    int i;

    printf("Environment variables\n");
    for (i = 0; environ[i] != NULL; i++)
        printf("\t%s\n", environ[i]);
    printf("Program parameters\n");
    for (i = 0; i<argc; i++)
        printf("\t%s\n", argv[i]);
    exit(0);
}
```

Listing 8-1: Echo command line arguments and print environment

8. 2   Spawning a New Process

Four basic system calls are provided for process manipulation: fork(), exec(), wait() and exit(). The fork() system call creates a new process and thus increases the total number of processes by one. The complementary function is exit(). It terminates the calling process, and thus decreases the total number of processes by one.

The wait() system call causes the caller to suspend until a child process stops or terminates. The exec() system call overlays a process with the code of another program. We will discuss this in the next section.

a. fork() system call – creates a new process

```
#include <sys/types.h>
#include <unistd.h>

pid_t fork();
```

The fork() system call causes the creation of a new process. The new (child) process is an exact copy (or clone) of the calling (parent) process except that

- the child process has a unique process number which does not match that of any active process, and

- the child process has a different parent process number.

Since a new (and near identical) process is created following a successful fork() system call, two processes seem to be returning from the call. fork() returns the child's process number to the parent. Since this information is not applicable to a child, it returns 0 to the child.

It is assumed that the appropriate code distinguishes between parent and child processes and guides subsequent execution accordingly. In the event of an erroneous situation, such as insufficient swap space or when a user process limit is reached, fork() returns -1 to indicate that a child process was not created.

As an almost exact copy of the parent process, the child process has the same variable locations. If the original source program had a variable x that was assigned location 1034 during compilation, the child process would also use the same mapping in which all references to variable x address that location.

Just after fork(), the child process will also have the same variable values. Note however, that these are in fact distinct instances. They are mapped onto distinct virtual pages in a machine. Subsequently, both processes are free to reassign to their variables and such side-effects have no effect on the other process.

The code in Listing 8-2 shows the effects of fork(). Note that the two occurrences of "After forktrial" show that the newly created child process even returns from a function call it "never made" but inherited.

```
void forktrial()
{
    int pid;

    pid = fork();
    if (pid == 0)
        printf("child process\n");
    else if (pid > 0)
        printf("parent process: child pid is %d\n", pid);
    else
        report_err("fork()");
}

main()
{
    printf("Before forktrial\n");
    forktrial();
    printf("After forktrial\n");
    exit(0);
}
```

Listing 8-2: fork() *test*

Note that the fork() does not define whether the parent or child proceeds first. This is left to the process scheduler. Such ordering would determine which printf() statement is executed. However, in this case, the output produced would be dependent of which buffer is flushed first.

Figure 8-1 illustrates a typical scenario with the fork() system call. When fork() is successful, parent and child processes are indicated by a positive and zero return values respectively. Here, irrelevant code fragments for each process are shaded.

b. exit() system call – terminates the calling process

```
void exit(int status);
```

The exit() system call terminates the calling process with an exit status code status. This call therefore does not return to the program. The parent of the terminated process may receive the status code via a wait() system call. By convention, zero is the status value to indicate normal termination.

It is useful that exit() also closes all opened file descriptors. This clean-up also occurs for opened streams from the *stdio* library package. In this case, the buffers of each stream are first flushed.

c. wait() system call – waits until a child process stops or terminates

```
int wait(int *status_loc);
```

If there are child processes, wait() sleeps until any child process terminates or stops. It returns that child's process number and stores the status code in the integer referenced by status_loc, unless it is NULL.

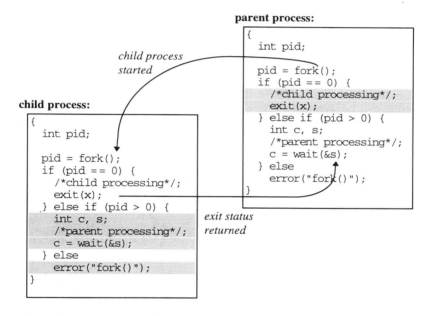

Figure 8-1: Relationship between fork()*,* wait()* and* exit()* system calls*

A process is terminated either because it executed exit(), or received a signal which it cannot handle. Signals might be user-generated, e.g. an interrupt signal (which is typically bound to the control-C key) or a kill signal, or be generated by the kernel due to some event, e.g. when a process executes an illegal instruction. The termination status pointed to by status_loc would correspond to the various termination conditions and is interpreted as follows:

- If the child process was terminated due to an `exit()`, the lower-order byte of `*status_loc` is zero, while the higher-order byte contains the child's exit status as indicated by the child's call to `exit()`.

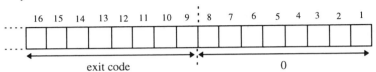

- If the child process was terminated due to a signal, the lower-order byte is non-zero. In this case, the rightmost seven bits of that value give the number of the signal which killed the child process. The leftmost bit of that byte indicates if a core dump was produced.

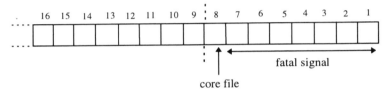

- If the child process was stopped, the lower-order byte contains `WSTOPFLG`, while the higher-order byte contains the number of the signal that caused the process to stop.

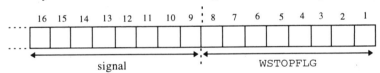

The `wait()` system call returns -1 immediately if there were no child processes. This could be because there never were any or because they were already waited for, or because they had been interrupted by a signal.

8.3   Executing Another Program

The `fork()` system call is not too useful on its own. It merely clones an existing process. Fortunately, it is augmented by a family of `exec()` system calls. This allows for another program to be loaded into the code space of the current process for execution.

a. exec() family of system calls – execute a program in a file

```
#include <unistd.h>

int execl(char *path, char *arg0, ..., char *argn, NULL);
int execv(char *path, char *argv[]);
int execle(char *path, char *arg0, ..., char *argn, NULL, char *envp[]);
```

The execl() system call and its other forms overlay the calling process with a new program image. The new program image is constructed from an executable file with pathname given by path. This file is either an executable object file, or a file of data for an interpreter. In the case of the latter, the interpreter is execed and the file of data used as the first argument to the interpreter.

Program parameters may be specified via strings arg0, ... argn. The use of the last NULL parameter signifies the end of the list. This is the standard method of passing a variable number of parameters to a function. Alternatively, the null-terminated string vector argv is used with the execv() form. This form is useful when the number of parameters cannot be determined at compile time (as in the execl() case).

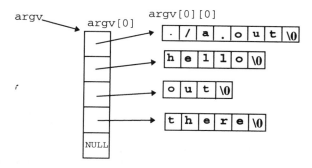

Figure 8-2: Character string vector of program arguments

Instead of the global default environ, a different environment may be specified via the null-terminated string vector envp for the execle() form.

There can be no return from a successful exec() call because the image of the calling process is already overlaid by the new program. The code in Listing 8-3 illustrates the use of execl().

```
#include <unistd.h>
#include <stdio.h>
main()
{
    printf("Before executing another program\n");
    execl("/bin/ls", "ls", "/bin", "/usr", NULL);
    printf("Previous program\n");
    exit(0);
}
```

Listing 8-3: exec() example

If the call to execl() is successful, the string "Previous program" is not printed because the corresponding machine code would have been overwritten by the code for /bin/ls. It is as though a program which executes execl() sacrifices itself so that a new program may be executed.

Other equivalent forms below accept parameters in a different form, but they give the same result of creating a new process.

```
int execve(char *path, char *argv[], char *envp[]);
int execlp(char *file, char *arg0, ..., char *argn, NULL);
int execvp(char *file, char *argv[]);
```

The execve() form is a cross between the execv() and execle() forms. The execlp() and execvp() forms are similar to the execl() and execv() forms except that a standard PATH search is performed to locate file.

The various forms in the exec() family may be summarised in Table 8-1.

System call	Argument format	Environment passing	Uses **PATH** search
execl()	parameter list	automatically inherited	no
execv()	array	automatically inherited	no
execle()	parameter list	explicit	no
execve()	array	explicit	no
execlp()	parameter list	automatically inherited	yes
execvp()	array	automatically inherited	yes

Table 8-1: exec() family of system calls

The exec() system call is often used in conjunction with fork(). A good instance is seen with program execution from a shell command interpreter. After it has interpreted the command line to decipher the program name and appropriate program arguments, it calls fork(). The newly created child process then executes an exec() system call, while the parent waits for the child to terminate. An essence of how the shell executes a program is shown in Listing 8-4.

```
void execute(char *prog, char *argv[])
{
    int pid;

    pid = fork();
    if (pid == 0) {
        execvp(prog, argv);
        report_err(prog);
    } else if (pid > 0)
        /* just wait for child process */
        wait(NULL);
    else
        report_err("fork()");
}

main()
{
    char *program = "ls";
    char *arguments[] = { "ls", "/etc", "." , NULL };

    printf("(assume: processing command line arguments)\n");
    execute(program, arguments);
    printf("after execute\n");
    exit(0);
}
```

Listing 8-4: Use of exec() with fork()

Most process attributes such as process ID, process owner and current working directory, are not changed by the exec() system call. File descriptors remain open and the process has the same indices to the same descriptors.

8. 4 Input/Output Redirection

It is often useful to place the output of commands like ls into a file. We can modify and recompile the source code for the ls command to write to a file instead of the screen. However, this is not a flexible approach. The UNIX strategy involves redirecting file descriptors instead.

A good example of input/output redirection is seen in a typical shell command interpreter. While the notations used in this context are "<" and ">", input/output redirection is in fact not a feature of the shell, but rather an example of redirecting file descriptors.

A simple way to achieve such redirection is to close the file descriptor which a program is expecting. It is then substituted with another by opening a new file. The code in Listing 8-5 shows how the standard output stream is closed. Another file SPOOL is opened to take the place of the former. The result is that SPOOL collects the output written by /bin/ls.

```
#include <unistd.h>
#include <stdio.h>
#include <sys/types.h>
#include <sys/stat.h>
#include <fcntl.h>

main()
{
    char *prog = "ls";
    char *argv[] = { "ls", "/etc", "." , NULL };
    int pid;

    printf("Before execute\n");
    pid = fork();
    if (pid == 0) {
        /* child process does all the following work */
        close(STDOUT_FILENO);
        if (creat("SPOOL", S_IRUSR|S_IWUSR|S_IRGRP|S_IROTH) == -1)
            report_err("SPOOL");
        execvp(prog, argv);
        report_err(prog);
    } else if (pid > 0)
        /* just wait for child process */
        wait(NULL);
    else
        report_err("fork()");
    printf("After execute\n");
}
```

Listing 8-5: Redirected file descriptor

The code used in the previous example is crude and will typically not be used. It gives the intended results only because of the nature of the situation: the program is very small and we know that the three file descriptors are opened: 0, 1 and 2 (STDIN_FILENO, STDOUT_FILENO and STDERR_FILENO).

The behaviour of creat() is such that it will use the lowest available descriptor number. After closing file descriptor 1, it becomes available for use. Since descriptor 0 is still open, opening SPOOL would thus use descriptor 1. It becomes a substitute for the former standard output stream to the terminal screen.

This method relies on knowing what file descriptors are available. The system calls creat() and open() always uses the lowest-value file description available. A more reliable method makes use of the dup2() library call so that we need not be concerned about which file descriptors are opened or closed.

a. dup() and dup2() system/library calls – duplicate a descriptor

```
int dup(int fd)

int dup2(int fd1, int fd2);
```

The dup() system call returns a new descriptor with the same characteristics as the existing file descriptor fd. This duplication implies that the new descriptor refers to

- the same file (or pipe),
- the same access mode, and
- the same file-pointer location.

The dup2() library call is a variant of dup(). It forces descriptor fd2 to be a duplicate of fd1. In this case, if fd2 is already open, it is first closed.

In both cases, a return result of −1 indicates an erroneous situation. The previous sample fragment in Listing 8-5 to illustrate redirection is improved in Listing 8-6. It is more robust by using dup2() since the file descriptor to be replaced may now be explicitly stated.

```c
#include <unistd.h>
#include <stdio.h>
#include <sys/types.h>
#include <sys/stat.h>
#include <fcntl.h>

main()
{
    char *prog = "ls";
    char *argv[] = { "ls", "/etc", "." , NULL };
    int pid;
    printf("Before execute\n");
    pid = fork();
    if (pid == 0) {
        /* child process does all the following work */
        int f;
        if ((f = creat("SPOOL", S_IRUSR|S_IWUSR|S_IRGRP|S_IROTH)) == -1)
            report_err("SPOOL");
        dup2(f, STDOUT_FILENO);
        close(f); /* after dup(), the original is no longer required */
        execvp(prog, argv);
        report_err(prog);
    } else if (pid > 0)
```

```
        /* just wait for child process */
        wait(NULL);
    else
        report_err("execute");
    printf("After execute\n");
    exit(0);
}
```

Listing 8-6: Redirected file descriptor via dup()

8. 5   Basic Interprocess Communication

A key characteristic of UNIX is that of program reuse. In the previous examples, the functionality of a separate program could be obtained by calling it using the exec() system call. In this section, we review another UNIX facility for combining the functionalities of several simpler programs.

A common complaint about many interactive commands (such as ls) is that their output scrolls too quickly off the screen. The solution of incorporating code to perform pagination is not ideal, since such effort must be duplicated in other applications which have similar requirements.

However, parts of the solution are already available. We have seen the use of the fork() and exec() system calls in the execution of another program. In our case, this would be an independent paginator program like the less command. In addition, we have seen the redirection of output through the modification of file descriptors, and how the output of the ls command may be redirected. The additional redirection is necessary to make less accept input from the output of the ls command.

The missing link is a connection between the output of the ls command to the input of the less command. UNIX provides a pipe feature for this. As with input/output redirection, the pipe facility as indicated by the notation "|" is not an inherent feature of the shell interpreter. Instead, this feature is offered by the UNIX kernel.

We recall that the child process created by fork() inherits the properties of its parent. In addition, exec() does not modify its file descriptors when it loads a new program. As with input/output redirection, the pipe feature also relies on making slight changes to the environment before invoking exec().

a. `pipe()` system call – creates an interprocess channel

```
#include <unistd.h>

int pipe(int fildes[2]);
```

The `pipe()` system call creates an input/output mechanism called a pipe and returns two file descriptors in `fildes[0]` and `fildes[1]`. A read from `fildes[0]` accesses the data written to `fildes[1]` on a first-in-first-out (FIFO) basis. For a bidirectional pipe, a read from `fildes[1]` also accesses the data written to `fildes[0]` on a FIFO basis.

This communication mechanism is demonstrated by using the program fragment in Listing 8-7. Data is written to `fdv[1]` and subsequently read from `fdv[0]`. While a pipe is typically used to connect two processes, a single process is used here for simplicity.

```
#include <unistd.h>
#include <stdio.h>
#include <sys/types.h>
#include <sys/stat.h>
#include <fcntl.h>

main()
{
    char *message = "hello world\n";
    int length = strlen(message);
    char buf[1024];
    int fdv[2];
    int n;

    if (pipe(fdv) == -1)
        report_err("pipe");

    if (write(fdv[1], message, length) != length)
        report_err("write to pipe");

    n = read(fdv[0], buf, length);
    if (n != length)
        report_err("read from pipe");
    write(STDOUT_FILENO, buf, n);
    exit(0);
}
```

Listing 8-7: Using a pipe

As a side issue, a pipe has a sufficiently big buffer (between 512 to 4096 bytes) to prevent the writing of a fairly short string (as in the above) from blocking. Writing to `fdv[1]` with a full buffer however would cause the process to block until the buffer is cleared by reading from fdv[0]. In this situation, deadlock occurs since reading from fdv[0] can only commence after the write operation. Similarly, if a pipe was unbuffered, writing to it would cause the caller to block until a reader clears it.

The program fragment in Listing 8-8 demonstrates how the output of the ls command may be piped to the less command. Note that the pipe is created *before* calling fork() to spawn the child process. This gives both parent and child processes access to the file descriptors associated with the pipe.

```
#include <unistd.h>
#include <stdio.h>

main()
{
    int pid;
    int pipev[2];

    if (pipe(pipev) == -1)
        report_err("pipe");

    pid = fork();
    if (pid == 0) {
        /* child process does all the following work */
        char *argv[] = { "ls", "-l", "/etc", "." , NULL };
        dup2(pipev[1], STDOUT_FILENO); /* redirect output of ls */
        close(pipev[0]); close(pipev[1]);
        execvp("ls", argv);
        report_err("ls");
    } else if (pid > 0) {
        dup2(pipev[0], STDIN_FILENO);  /* redirect input of less */
        close(pipev[1]); close(pipev[0]);
        execlp("less", "less", NULL);
        report_err("less");
    } else
        report_err("fork");

    printf("finish\n");
}
```

Listing 8-8: Communicating via a pipe

In Listing 8-8, the child process makes the writing end of pipev the new standard output descriptor to execute the ls command. In the same way, the parent makes the reading end of pipev the new standard input descriptor for less to read the output of ls.

Note that in this case, the last printf statement is never executed because the parent process "committed suicide" after executing the less command. This however is not the typical form of usage of command shells. The usual pattern of usage is that output from the parent is written to the pipe; and the child process invokes the paginator to read from the other end of the pipe. This is illustrated in Listing 8-9.

```
#include <unistd.h>
#include <stdio.h>

main()
{
    int pid;
    int pipev[2];

    if (pipe(pipev) == -1)
        report_err("pipe");

    pid = fork();
    if (pid == 0) {
        dup2(pipev[0], STDIN_FILENO);   /* redirect input of less */
        close(pipev[1]); close(pipev[0]);
        execlp("less", "less", NULL);
        report_err("less");
    } else if (pid > 0) {
        int i;
        FILE *pfd = fdopen(pipev[1], "w");

        close(pipev[0]);
        for (i = 0; i < 100; i++)
            fprintf(pfd, "this is test line  %d\n", i);
        fclose(pfd);
        wait(NULL);
    } else
        report_err("fork");

    printf("finish\n");
    exit(0);
}
```

Listing 8-9: Typical use of pipe

Using pipes for basic process communication, as in the above program fragment, is simplified by the popen() and pclose() *stdio* library routines.

b. popen() and pclose() library calls – initiate and close a pipe

```
#include <stdio.h>

FILE *popen(char *command, char *type);

int pclose (FILE *stream);
```

The popen() library call creates a pipe between the calling process and the command to be executed. command consists of a shell command line. type is the operation mode, similar to that used in fopen(): either "r" for reading from or "w" for writing to the pipe.

If the operation mode is "w", popen() returns a stream to write to the standard input stream of command. If the operation mode is "r", popen() returns a stream to read from the standard output stream of command. In both cases, a NULL result indicates that the pipe was not successfully created.

A stream opened by popen() should be closed by pclose(). It closes the pipe and waits for the associated process to terminate. It then returns the exit status of the command. This pattern is outlined in Listing 8-10.

```
#include <stdio.h>

main()
{
    int i;
    FILE *pfd;

    pfd = popen("less", "w");
    if (pfd == NULL)
        report_err("less");
    for (i = 0; i < 100; i++)
        fprintf(pfd, "this is test line  %d\n", i);
    pclose(pfd);
    printf("finish\n");
    exit(0);
}
```

Listing 8-10: Creating a pipe via popen()

8. 6   Process Characteristics

So far, we have seen how a new process is created, how file descriptors could be altered and how a process might communicate with another program via a pipe. We now continue by examining other process characteristics.

a. `getpid()` and `getppid()` system calls – return process IDs

```
#include <sys/types.h>
#include <unistd.h>

pid_t getpid(void);

pid_t getppid(void);
```

The `getpid()` system call returns the process ID of the caller. The `getppid()` system call returns the process ID of the caller's parent.

b. `chdir()` and `fchdir()` system calls – change the working directory

```
#include <unistd.h>

int chdir(char *path);

int fchdir(int fildes);
```

The `chdir()` system call causes the current working directory to be changed to that specified by the string `path`. Alternatively, `fchdir()` achieves the same effect, but the target directory is specified via an opened descriptor `fildes`.

A current working directory must be accessible to a process. `chdir()` and `fchdir()` return 0 to signify success, and -1 otherwise.

c. `getuid()` and `getgid()` – get the real-user and real-group IDs

```
#include <sys/types.h>
#include <unistd.h>

uid_t getuid(void);

gid_t getgid(void);
```

`getuid()` returns the real-user ID of the calling process. Similarly, `getgid()` returns the real-group ID of the calling process. The real-user ID is an attribute of each process. It identifies the owner of the process and the person logged in.

d. `geteuid()` and `getegid()` – get effective-user and effective-group IDs

```
#include <sys/types.h>
#include <unistd.h>

uid_t geteuid(void);

gid_t getegid(void);
```

`geteuid()` returns the effective-user ID of the calling process. Similarly, `getegid()` returns the effective-group ID of the calling process. These effective values are those that are matched with access permissions when files are opened for either reading, writing or execution.

8. 7 *setuid* Programs

The UNIX file system maintains ownership and access permissions of each file. The kernel allows file access based on the effective-user and effective-group IDs of each process. However, there are times when users must perform a privileged but controlled task. An example of such a task is password maintenance.

- A user is normally not given write permissions on the password file. Otherwise, he might change his user ID to that of root's, or his enemy's encrypted password. However, when changing a password, a user is temporarily given the permission to update the password file.

- The permission to update the password must be controlled so that a user is restricted to only changing the password file, and even then, only his own password.

The above criterion are implemented as follows:

- Privileged commands are implemented as *setuid* programs. During the execution of a *setuid* program, the user is given a temporary switch of identity. This allows for updates on a file which is not owned by the process and thus not normally readable and/or writable. These privileges are withdrawn when the *setuid* program terminates.

- Since privileges are only granted during the execution of the *setuid* program, restrictions on what operations are allowable are checked by the *setuid* program itself.

Typically, the real and effective IDs are identical when executing normal utilities like the `vi` editor. Since `/etc/passwd` is read-only to mortal users, write privileges are required when a password modification is attempted. The `passwd` command is said to be a *setuid* program. Note that its file status is different from commands like `vi`:

```
-r-xr-xr-x   5 bin      bin       226844 Sep 27  1993 /usr/bin/vi
-r-sr-xr-x   1 root     sys        11492 Sep 27  1993 /usr/bin/passwd
```

We have already seen that a shell executes a program by first calling `fork()` to clone itself. This provides an additional thread of execution. The child process then calls `exec()` to load the program. In the meantime, the calling process waits for the child's completion.

setuid (or *setgid*) programs are indicated by an "s" instead of an "x" in the owner (or group) execute-permission column. In this situation, the `exec()` system call saves the effective-user (or group) ID, and makes the effective-user (or group) ID that of the owner (or group) of the program. Thus, a process which runs a command like `passwd` has root as the effective-user ID until it exits.

8. 8   Changing User and Group IDs

Closely related to *setuid* programs are system calls to change the user and group IDs of the calling process. Security loopholes often occur because these features are not carefully considered.

a. `setuid()`, `setgid()`, `setegid()`, `seteuid()` system calls – set user/group IDs

```
#include <sys/types.h>
#include <unistd.h>

int setuid(uid_t uid);
int setgid(gid_t gid);
int seteuid(uid_t euid);
int setegid(gid_t egid);
```

The `setuid()` system call sets the real-user ID, effective-user ID, and saved-user ID of the calling process to `uid`. Similarly, the `setgid()` system call sets the real-group ID, effective-group ID, and saved-group ID of the calling process to `gid`.

The `seteuid()` and `setegid()` system calls only set the effective-user and group IDs respectively of the calling process to `euid` and `egid`.

Since these system calls change user and group IDs, they potentially allow a user to assume the identity of any user, making file-access permissions redundant. The UNIX kernel must thus ensure that these are only permissible under certain conditions. The following rules for such calls are implemented by the kernel to prevent abuse:

- If the effective-user ID of the process-calling setuid() is the superuser[1], the real, effective, and saved-user IDs are set to the uid parameter.

  If the effective-user ID of the process-calling setuid() is not the superuser, but uid is either the real or saved-user IDs, the effective-user ID is set to uid.

- The seteuid() system call behaves like setuid() for the non-superuser.

  For the superuser, seteuid() affects only the effective-user ID and differs from setuid(), which affects all three.

- The setuid() and seteuid() system calls will fail for the non-superuser when uid is not the real or saved-user ID.

- The corresponding behaviour for groups apply to the setgid() and setegid() system calls and group IDs.

The above rules place the restriction that only the superuser may change the real-user and group IDs.

b. The su command

The su program is an interesting example of how the setuid() and setgid() system calls could be useful. Briefly, it allows an identity switch to a specified user and then spawns a new shell. This command is useful when a separate login session is physically not possible, or when the session is needed temporarily.

Note that it executes with the effective-user ID as superuser:

```
-r-sr-xr-x   1 root      sys        14036 Sep 27  1993 /bin/su
```

To prevent abuse, su prompts for the password of the assumed user. If user authentication is successful, it calls setuid() and setgid() with the appropriate user ID. These calls succeed because su executes as root. It then calls exec() to overlay the process with the default shell.

c. The login procedure

When a new terminal session is requested, a process is created by root to prompt for the login name and corresponding password. If user authentication is successful, appropriate log files are updated to reflect the new user session. Subsequently, process characteristics are altered to that of the user.

---

[1] The superuser, root or system administrator takes on the user ID of zero. Processes with this user ID tag are not subject to the safeguards or restrictions implemented by the kernel.

The setuid() and setgid() system calls are used to change the owner and group of the processes to the values in the user's password entry[2]. The working directory of the process is also changed to the user's home directory. Finally, the process execs the login shell and the user thus has a login session.

8. 9 Summary

This chapter has reviewed the following facilities offered by the UNIX system for process creation and program execution:

§ Process creation and termination

    fork(), exit(), wait()

§ Program execution

    execl(), execv(), execle(), execve(), execlp(), execvp()

§ Input/output redirection

    dup(), dup2()

§ Pipe communication channel

    pipe(), popen(), pclose()

§ Process attributes

    getpid(), getppid(), chdir(), fchdir(), getuid(), getgid(), geteuid(), getegid()

§ Privileged programs

    setuid(), setgid(), setegid(), seteuid()

Comprehensive information on obtaining process attributes may be found in the proc(4) man page.

---

[2] User authentication, password details and user information are discussed in the next chapter.

8. 10   Exercises

1. Extend the editor such that a sequence of lines may be filtered through any UNIX command. One might specify that n lines from the editing buffer be used as input for a specific command. Subsequently, output is redirected back into the editing buffer. This is a simple way of extending the editing capabilities of the editor.

2. Copy the id command into your directory and set its *setuid* bit on. Get another user to run the program and compare the results with those produced by the original version.

3. Write a "friend" program which allows trusted friends to assume your ID. Describe desirable security features and show how their actions might be restricted.

9

Administrative Information

In the previous two chapters, we discussed the basic facilities for manipulating two important classes of UNIX entities, namely files and processes. Before proceeding further, it is useful to look at how administrative information is stored, and the associated library routines to access it. For example, we often need to map user IDs to login names and home directories.

We will also examine some miscellaneous routines for reading passwords, accessing environment variables, performing time-format conversion and creating temporary files.

9. 1   User Account Information

Each user on a UNIX system is assigned a unique username and user ID number. The username is a convenient string representation for humans. UNIX entities, like files and processes, are tagged internally with the user ID number instead. The mapping of usernames to user identities are contained in the password file /etc/passwd. Each user has a line in the password file:

userid:*password*:*uid*:*gid*:*gcos-field*:*home-dir*:*login-shell*

The information in the password file is accessed frequently and various library routines have been implemented to conveniently accomplish this. For example, the routines getpwnam() and getpwuid() access a line in the password file by using the username and user ID as search keys.

Since each field in a password entry is separated by a colon, the routines also parse the line and place them into separate fields of a `struct passwd` variable. Password file information and associated field names are enumerated in Table 9-1.

Field	Remarks	**passwd** field names
userid	username	char *pw_name
password	encrypted password for user	char *pw_passwd
uid	user ID number	int pw_uid
gid	group ID number	int pw_gid
gcos-field	information about user (e.g. full name)	char *pw_gecos
home-dir	user's home directory	char *pw_dir
login-shell	user's login shell	char *pw_shell

Table 9-1: Fields in password entry

a. `getpwnam()`, `getpwuid()` library calls – search for matching password entry

```
#include <pwd.h>

struct passwd *getpwnam(char *name);
struct passwd *getpwuid(uid_t uid);
```

The `getpwnam()` library routine searches for a password entry whose username is `name`. If one is found, it copies and assembles the relevant information into a `struct passwd` variable and returns its address. If a matching entry is not found, it returns NULL. The `getpwuid()` routine is similar, but it searches for an entry whose UID field matches `uid`.

b. User information program

The program fragment in Listing 9-1 shows how information about users may be obtained:

```
#include <stdio.h>
#include <pwd.h>

main(int argc, char *argv[])
{
    int i;
    struct passwd *pass;

    for (i=1; i<argc; i++) {
        pass = getpwnam(argv[i]);
```

```
        if (pass)
            printf("login: %s\nName:%s\nUID=%d\n",
                            pass->pw_name, pass->pw_gecos, pass->pw_uid);
        else
            fprintf(stderr, "%s does not exist\n", argv[i]);
    }
    exit(0);
}
```

Listing 9-1: Reading password file information

c. **identify program**

The program fragment in Listing 9-2 shows how details of the owner of a process may be obtained.

```
#include <stdio.h>
#include <pwd.h>

main()
{
    int i;
    struct passwd *pass;

    pass = getpwuid(getuid());
    if (!pass)
        report_err("getpwuid()");
    printf("you are %s\n", pass->pw_gecos);
    exit(0);
}
```

Listing 9-2: Reading process information

When many entries in the password file require processing, it is more efficient to read entries sequentially.

d. **setpwent(), getpwent(), endpwent() library calls** – read the password file

```
#include <pwd.h>

void setpwent();
struct passwd *getpwent();
void endpwent();
```

The library routine `getpwent()` is used to read each password entry sequentially. It returns `NULL` when there are no more entries. Otherwise, it returns a pointer to a `struct passwd` as with `getpwnam()`.

The routine `setpwent()` should always be called to initialise reading from the first password entry. Similarly, `endpwent()` is used to indicate that no more password calls are required and that the associated file descriptor may be deallocated.

9.2 Passwords and Password Encryption

User passwords in UNIX are encrypted using a one-way hashing encryption algorithm. The resulting encrypted form is stored in the password field of an unshadowed[1] password entry. It is visible because in principle the password cannot be regenerated from the encrypted form.

Login validation consists of repeating the encryption process and comparing the result with what is stored in the password entry. Figure 9-1 provides an overview of the processing involved.

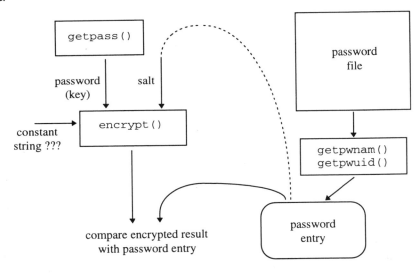

Figure 9-1: Password encryption

---

[1] The unshadowed scheme gives read access to the encrypted password. This however has been the target of crackers who attempt good password guesses and compare the result of the encryption with what is stored in the password entry. The shadowed scheme is an improvement in that user information is kept separately from encypted passwords. While the user information is still readable, the password is now only readable to privileged programs.

Password encryption works by using the user's password as the key to repeatedly encrypt a constant string. An additional two-character salt string is used to modify the hashing algorithm.

a. `getpass()` library routine – reads the password file

```
#include <stdlib.h>

char *getpass(char *prompt);
```

The library routine `getpass()` is used to read a password. It issues the prompt `prompt` on the standard error stream, turns off terminal echoing and reads up to a newline or end-of-file (EOF) from the terminal.

If successful, it returns a pointer to a null-terminated string of at most eight characters. Otherwise, if `getpass()` cannot read from the terminal, it returns NULL to indicate failure.

b. `crypt()` library routine – encrypts a password string

```
#include <crypt.h>

char *crypt(char *key, char *salt);
```

The library routine `crypt()` is used to encrypt a user's password. When a password is initially selected, `crypt()` is given a randomly selected two-character salt. The original password is supplied as `key`. `crypt()` returns the encrypted form, preserving the salt as the first two characters. Subsequent password validation must use this salt.

c. Password-validation program

The program fragment in Listing 9-3 demonstrates the use of the `getpass()` and `crypt()` functions for password validation.

```
#include <stdio.h>
#include <stdlib.h>
#include <pwd.h>
#include <crypt.h>

main()
{
    struct passwd *pwent;
    char *clearpw, *encrypted;

    pwent = getpwuid(getuid());
    if (!pwent)
        report_err("getpwuid()");
    clearpw = getpass("password:");
    if (clearpw) {
        char salt[3];

        strncpy(salt, pwent->pw_passwd, 2);
        encrypted = crypt(clearpw, salt);
        if (strcmp(encrypted, pwent->pw_passwd) != 0) {
            printf("Invalid password\n");
            exit(1);
        }
        printf("OK\n");
    }
    exit(0);
}
```

Listing 9-3: Password validation

9. 3   Time Functions

UNIX maintains a real-time clock. For administrative purposes, it is convenient to put one or more time stamps on UNIX entities. We have seen that each file has three time stamps in its *inode* block: the times of creation, modification and last access. Similarly, each process has a time stamp of when it was started.

There are three basic representation formats for time: time_t, struct tm and ASCII strings. A time_t quantity is the number of seconds since 00:00:00 GMT January 1, 1970 (also known as the Epoch). The representation is convenient for storage, but not for selective access. Instead, struct tm is used when selective access is necessary.

struct tm fields	Remarks
`int   tm_sec;`	seconds after the minute [0-61]
`int   tm_min;`	minutes after the hour [0-59]
`int   tm_hour;`	hours since midnight [0-23]
`int   tm_mday;`	day of the month [1-31]
`int   tm_mon;`	months since January [0-11]
`int   tm_year;`	years since 1900
`int   tm_wday;`	days since Sunday [0-6]
`int   tm_yday;`	days since January 1 [0-365]
`int   tm_isdst;`	daylight savings time flag: It is positive if daylight savings time is in effect, zero if daylight savings time is not in effect, and negative if the information is not available.

Table 9-2: `struct tm` *fields*

The ASCII string representation is used when we want to print a time out in a standard format. The routines `ctime()`, `asctime()`, `localtime()` and `gmtime()` allow for format conversion between the three forms discussed above. Their relationship is outlined in Figure 9-2.

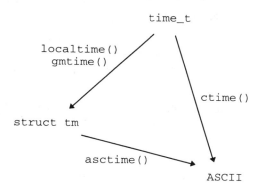

Figure 9-2: Time conversion routines

a. `ctime()`, `asctime()`, `localtime()`, `gmtime()` **library functions** – convert between time formats

```
#include <time.h>

char *ctime(time_t *clock);
char *asctime(struct tm *tm);
struct tm *localtime(time_t *clock);
struct tm *gmtime(time_t *clock);
```

The functions `ctime()` and `asctime()` convert from `time_t` and `struct tm` representations to ASCII. The functions `localtime()` and `gmtime()` convert from `time_t` to `struct tm` representations. `localtime()` conversion takes into account time zones and daylight savings. `gmtime()` leaves the result in Coordinated Universal Time (UTC).

9. 4   Using Temporary Files

Many applications in UNIX rely on temporary files. In fact, the `/tmp` directory is specially designated for temporary files. It is convenient to create temporary files there so that periodic spring-cleaning is easily achieved by wiping off the whole directory. Furthermore, where `/tmp` is allocated a separate disk partition, it need not be backed-up.

When a user replies a mail message, a mail reader typically copies the original message into a temporary file. The user composes the reply by editing the temporary file. When its contents are finalised, it is sent via the `sendmail` program. This strategy applies to news messages as well.

The main concern with temporary files is potential name conflict with multiple program invocations. Since process IDs are unique, a solution would be to include the process ID as part of a temporary filename.

a. `tmpfile()` **library routine** – creates temporary files

```
#include <stdio.h>

FILE *tmpfile();
```

The `tmpfile()` library routine creates a temporary file using a name generated by the `tmpnam()` routine and opens it for read/write access. It returns the resultant `FILE` pointer. A `NULL` pointer is returned if the file cannot be opened.

In addition, the file is automatically deleted when the process using it is terminated or when the file is closed.

9. 5   Using Environment Variables

It is common practice to pass customisation parameters via environment variables. For example, interactive programs such as pine and less look at the environment variable EDITOR for the user's favourite editor when they require one. The alternative method of passing parameters via command-line arguments is tedious if it must be repeatedly specified.

a. getenv() and putenv() library routines – read and set environment variables

```
#include <stdlib.h>

char *getenv(char *name);

int putenv(char *def);
```

The environment of a process is represented by a list of strings with the form:

sym=value

The library routine getenv() searches the environment for a string with *sym* equal to name. If a match is found, it returns a pointer to value. Otherwise, it returns NULL.

The library routine putenv() performs the complementary function. def also has the string form as above, and it becomes part of the environment. An effect of the new definition is that any string in the environment defining sym is removed.

9. 6   Summary

The following routines were discussed in this chapter:

§   password file access

setpwent(), getpwent(), endpwent()

§   user information

getpwnam(), getpwuid()

§   password validation
    `getpass(), crypt()`

§   time-format conversion
    `ctime(), asctime(), localtime(), gmtime()`

§   temporary files
    `tmpfile()`

§   environment variables
    `getenv(), putenv()`

Further details of the password file structure may be found in the `passwd(4)` man page. Password encryption routines are found in the `crypt(3)` man page. Time functions are available in the `ctime(3)` man page.

9. 7   Exercises

1. Modify the browser file opening routines so that it takes the FILEPATH environment variable into consideration. While PATH contains the directory list of executable programs, FILEPATH contains the directory list to search for input files. Just as for PATH, it might be set to

    ```
    $ export FILEPATH=~user:~user/data:~user/testdata
    ```

    When a filename specified by a relative pathname is to be opened, the directory list is searched for the first location with the specified name.

2. Implement a terminal-locking program to secure a terminal during quick trips to the toilet. While it prevents others from using your account in your absence, a correct password will let you continue your session. An added feature is that it must release the terminal for use if you do not return in 15 minutes.

10

Signals and Exceptions

A signal is an asynchronous notification of an event. It is sent to a process when an associated event occurs, and that process may specify a course of action when a signal is received. Signals behave much like software interrupts. Examples of events which generate signals include hardware faults and timer expiration, and user-generated signals, such as those sent by the `kill` command or the interrupt key, which are used to prematurely abort an operation or process.

Most applications would at least need to deal with the interrupt signal so that appropriate finalisation code may be invoked before exiting. Actions might involve the deleting of unwanted temporary files, or adding of an entry into the system log.

In more sophisticated applications, an asynchronous signal notification relieves the program from continually polling for the event in question. In a polling situation, the particular condition must be checked at *every* instance when there is a possibility of an occurrence of that event.

```
while (still_searching) {
    if (interrupt_key) {
        stop_searching;
        clean_up;
        break;
    }
    ... /* search proper */
}
```

An asynchronous signal notification scheme provides a neater and more efficient alternative. It could also simplify control-flow issues. The following fragment shows the paradigm for handling asynchronous events. It is not necessarily C syntax or semantics.

```
on interrupt, jump end_search;
while (still_searching) {
    ... /* search proper */
}
end_search:
```

Here, the event and relevant action are stated at the start of processing. Execution may then proceed without concern about the event in question. But whenever the interrupt key is pressed, an implicit jump out of the searching loop (to the label site end_search) aborts the search operation.

The subsequent sections discuss the features of asynchronous signals in UNIX and how a routine may be installed as an event handler. We also see how exceptions may be handled.

10. 1   Sending Signals to Processes

The kill command in UNIX is often used to terminate a background process. In such a situation, we would typically confirm the ID of the unwanted process via a ps command before we terminate the process via kill -15, or kill -9 if the former did not do the job.

```
$ ps
    PID TTY        TIME COMD
 11775 pts/67     0:04 bash
 12319 pts/67     0:00 a.out
 12583 pts/67     0:01 ps
$ kill -15 12319
$ ps
    PID TTY        TIME COMD
 11775 pts/67     0:04 bash
 12319 pts/67     0:00 a.out
 12601 pts/67     0:01 ps
```

A subsequent ps command is then issued to confirm if the process had in fact terminated. In the sample session above, it had not, and kill is repeated with -9.

```
$ kill -9 12319
$ ps
    PID TTY          TIME COMD
  11775 pts/67       0:04 bash
  12601 pts/67       0:01 ps
```

The reason why a.out might not have terminated will be evident later in the chapter. For the moment, suffice it to note that the kill command sends various signals to a process and with various outcomes.

The kill command may also be used on foreground processes which refuse to terminate via the interrupt key. If the shell supports job control, the foreground process might be suspended and the kill command may then be used. Alternatively, the kill command may be issued from a second login session at another terminal.

However, the kill command is a misnomer. It does not always kill a process and is not only used for terminating a process. In general, it sends a specific signal to target processes. Whether or not the signal terminates the process depends on which signal is sent, and how the process had planned to respond to it.

The popular signals which a process might encounter are summarised in Table 10-1. The name and value columns give the symbolic name and the actual represented value of each signal. The event column describes the situation in which the signal is sent. Lastly, the default action column shows how a process will typically respond. Since such a general response might be inappropriate, a process may choose to overwrite it with a more appropriate action.

Name	Value	Event	Default action
SIGHUP	1	Hangup: The SIGHUP signal is sent to a process when its associated terminal has been disconnected, or when its login shell terminates.	Exit
SIGINT	2	Interrupt: The SIGINT signal is sent from the keyboard driver, in response to the interrupt key, to the current foreground process.	Exit
SIGQUIT	3	Quit: The SIGQUIT signal is sent from the keyboard driver, in response to the quit key, to the current foreground process.	Exit with core
SIGILL	4	Illegal Instruction: The SIGILL signal is sent to a process when an illegal instruction is encountered.	Exit with core
SIGTRAP	5	Trace/Breakpoint Trap: The SIGTRAP signal indicates an implementation-defined fault.	Exit with core
SIGABRT	6	Abort: The SIGABRT signal signifies abnormal termination, and is sent to the process calling abort().	Exit with core

Name	Value	Event	Default action
SIGEMT	7	Emulation Trap: The SIGEMT signal indicates an implementation-defined fault.	Exit with core
SIGFPE	8	Arithmetic Exception: The SIGFPE signal is sent to a process during an arithmetic error (e.g. division by 0, or floating-point exception).	Exit with core
SIGKILL	9	Kill: The SIGKILL signal is sent to terminate a process. Since it cannot be caught or ignored, it results in a definite kill.	Exit
SIGBUS	10	Bus Error: The SIGBUS signal is sent to the process which attempts an illegal memory reference.	Exit with core
SIGSEGV	11	Segmentation Fault: The SIGSEGV signal is sent to the process which attempted an illegal memory reference.	Exit with core
SIGSYS	12	Bad System Call: The SIGSYS signal is sent in response to a bad argument when entering supervisory mode.	Exit with core
SIGPIPE	13	Broken Pipe: The SIGPIPE signal is generated when a process writes to a pipe whose reader has terminated.	Exit
SIGALRM	14	Alarm Clock: The SIGALRM signal notifies a process that the time interval set by alarm() has expired.	Exit
SIGTERM	15	Terminate: The SIGTERM signal is the default signal from the kill command.	Exit
SIGUSR1	16	User Signal 1: The SIGUSR1 signal is user-defined, and may be associated with user-defined events.	Exit
SIGUSR2	17	User Signal 2: The SIGUSR2 signal is user-defined, and may be associated with user-defined events.	Exit
SIGCHLD	18	Child Status Changed: The SIGWCHLD signal is sent to the parent process whose child's status has changed	Ignore
SIGWINCH	20	Window Size Change: The SIGWINCH signal is sent to the process whose window size had changed.	Ignore

Table 10-1: Common signals

10. 2 Responding to a Signal

There are three different responses a process may adopt when a signal is received:

- apply the default action,

- ignore the signal altogether, or

- catch the signal by providing an appropriate action.

The default action is that which is usually appropriate to most programs, as shown in the above table. This is often to exit with or without the core file. This core file is analogous to a program corpse. It is the process image left over in memory when a process dies. Other default actions for signals include stopping the process or ignoring the signal.

Where the default action is not to ignore the signal, the programmer may choose to ignore it anyway. However, this might not always be the sensible course of action. For example, ignoring a segmentation fault caused by referencing an invalid pointer merely produces undefined results. Unless care is taken to ignore such results, carrying on with program execution under such situations will lead to non-deterministic behaviour.

Alternatively, the program can respond to an event by supplying a signal handler in the form of a function. In this case, a signal causes the process to be interrupted while the signal-handler function is invoked. On returning from the signal handler, the process resumes execution from where it previously left off.

a. signal() system call – signal management for process

```
#include <signal.h>

void (*signal (int sig, void (*disp)(int)))(int);
```

The signal() system call modifies the action (or disposition) of a signal for the executing process. The signal concerned is specified by sig. The disposition disp is either SIG_DFL, SIG_IGN or a pointer to the function to handle the signal. This corresponds to the three previously outlined possible responses: adopt the default action, ignore the signal, or invoke the user-defined handler routine.

If successful, signal() returns the previous disposition for sig. Otherwise, it returns SIG_ERR and sets errno to indicate the error. This description gives a clue to interpreting the rather complex declaration of signal().

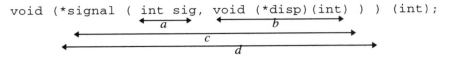

Figure 10-1: Interpreting void (*signal(int sig, void (*disp) (int)))(int)

Fragments *a* and *b* in Figure 10-1 describe parameters `sig` and `disp` respectively: `sig` is an integer signal representation, while `disp` is a pointer to the new handler function which is expecting an integer argument, but does not return any result. They make up the formal parameters of the function `signal` as indicated by fragment *c*.

If we simplified the original declarator by substituting the fragment with just `fc`, fragment *d* simply becomes:

```
void (*fc)(int);
```

This denotes a pointer to a function which expects an integer parameter. Thus, while `signal()` sets up a new handler, it also returns the old one. By breaking down code fragments in the original `signal()` declarator, we are able to confirm that the notation does specify that `signal()` installs a new disposition, and in so doing returns the previous disposition. It is therefore not surprising that the signatures of `disp()` and `fc()` are similar.

Listing 10-1 shows a skeleton view of how a signal handler might be installed.

```
#include <stdio.h>
#include <signal.h>

void handler(int sig)
{
    printf("signal %d caught\n", sig);
}

main()
{
    void (*older_handler)(int);

    older_handler = signal(SIGINT, handler);/* setup new disposition */
    /* processing */
    ...
    signal(SIGINT, older_handler); /* restore old disposition */
}
```

Listing 10-1: Framework for installing a signal handler

Since signal() returns the former disposition, it might be saved. The signal disposition may then be restored by installing the older handler.

For System V systems, a signal handler installed via signal() is reset to SIG_DFL after the signal is caught. In this case, the program terminates (default action) on receiving a second SIGINT signal. However, with BSD systems, a signal handler installed in the same way remains installed even after the signal is caught.

For situations in System V where a signal handler should remain installed after the signal is caught, it might be reinstalled as in Listing 10-2.

```
#include <stdio.h>
#include <signal.h>

void handler(int sig)
{
    signal(SIGINT, handler); /* re-install handler */
    printf("signal %d caught\n", sig);
}

main()
{
    void (*older_handler)(int);

    older_handler = signal(SIGINT, handler); /* setup new disposition */
    /* processing */
    ...
    signal(SIGINT, older_handler); /* restore old disposition */
}
```

Listing 10-2: Reinstalling a signal handler

There is however, a slight timing problem in this solution. Since the signal's disposition is reset to SIGDFL, a (very quick) SIGINT can arrive before the handler is reinstalled and will terminate the program (which is the default action of SIGINT).

The sigset() system call provides a reliable method for this situation.

b. **sigset() system call** — signal management for process

```
#include <signal.h>

void (*sigset (int sig, void (*disp)(int)))(int);
```

sigset() provides the same functionality as signal(). However, the signal's disposition is not reset to SIGDFL after the signal is caught.

Incidentally, the earlier program fragment has a user-defined SIGINT disposition which merely prints out a message. The process therefore cannot rely on the default action of SIGINT to terminate. Instead, another signal such as SIGQUIT, whose default action is to terminate the process, should be used. Alternatively, the sure-kill signal SIGKILL might be used, since it cannot be ignored or caught by installing a new disposition. This ensures that there is still a means of terminating a process whose signal disposition has not been correctly installed.

Note that like most other process characteristics, signal dispositions are also inherited by child processes during a fork() system call. However, when the process image is overlaid by another program via the exec() system call, user-defined signal handlers will also be overwritten. As a result of this situation, signals that are caught by user-defined handlers are set to the default dispositions after an exec() system call.

10. 3   The Role of Signal Handlers

There are three reasons why we might want to catch a signal such as SIGINT. Firstly, we do not want our program to be terminated due to (accidental) use of the interrupt key. In the case of an editor program, aborting prematurely would lose the contents of the file under edit. A well-designed application must take such circumstances into consideration. A possible solution would be to set the signal disposition for SIGINT to SIG_IGN.

Secondly, we might want a program to terminate on receiving SIGINT, but only after appropriate finalisation and housekeeping actions have been carried out. Such actions might be to delete unwanted or temporary files, to complete logging information, or to notify other processes about the intention to terminate.

Yet another possibility is for the SIGINT signal to merely abort an operation rather than the process. For example, a program might repeatedly prompt for a user-query request, and then perform a corresponding retrieval operation. A user might abort a retrieval which does not seem to be making good progress, but still continue within the query/retrieval cycle. Such control-flow issues will be further elaborated on in subsequent sections.

10. 4   Exceptions

While goto statements are often discouraged in programming classes, their use need not always be inappropriate. In fact, goto statements can sometimes improve program structure. They have remained in most imperative languages. goto statements generally serve two purposes:

- They provide a neat way of retreating from error situations without requiring extra tests and flags.

- They allow for quick exits from nested block structures, a feature that is convenient in a language like Pascal.

However, the need for non-local branches as in Pascal does not arise in C since C does not provide for nested functions. But the need for non-local branching based on the dynamic call graph remains. Consider the following two program structures in Figure 10-2.

```
a()                         a()
{                           {
   x:                          goto x;  ....  goto y;
}                           }
b()                         b()
{                           {
    goto x;                     a();
                                x:
}                           }
main()                      main()
{                           {
    b();                        b();
                                y:
}                           }
```

Figure 10-2: Non-local branches

While both are invalid C fragments, the first case is obviously badly written and lacks clear semantics. Firstly, memory allocation for local variables is not implied by branching into a block. Secondly, the appropriate action at the end of function a() is unclear since there is no return address associated with the branch instruction. More rules and mechanisms must therefore be incorporated for this sort of non-local branching to be viable and useful.

On the other hand, the non-local branches to x and y in the second case may be seen as quick exits back to caller functions which are active and whose activation records are still on the stack. It implies that storage allocations have previously been performed for the destination block. What is left are deallocations of intervening blocks. Branching from function a() to site y in function main() implies deallocation of local variables of function b().

While non-local branching in the second case is logical, the two cases cannot be syntactically distinguished. This is one reason why non-local branches are not allowed. In practice, however, the effect of the second case may be achieved via the library functions, setjmp() and longjmp().

a. `setjmp()` and `longjmp()` library calls – allow for non-local branches

```
#include <setjmp.h>

int setjmp(jmp_buf env);

void longjmp(jmp_buf env, int val);
```

The `setjmp()` library call saves the stack environment in a data structure `env` of type `jmp_buf`. Control may then be returned to the location after the `setjmp()` by calling `longjmp()` with the corresponding `jmp_buf` variable.

When called directly, `setjmp()` always returns 0. This distinguishes it from the other case when `longjmp()` returns control to it. When this happens, `setjmp()` would **seem** to return a non-zero value as specified by `val` in the corresponding call of `longjmp()`. Even if a number of active function calls separate the original call to `setjmp()` and `longjmp()`, it would appear as if all intervening calls were terminated. A call to `longjmp()` therefore does not return. Note that the caller of `setjmp()` must not have returned before the corresponding call to `longjmp()` is made.

Listing 10-3 provides an example of how a non-local branch is achieved. It may be viewed as consisting of three parts:

- an initialisation code portion which needs to be executed only once, and not for each restart occasion,

- a restart location which expects to receive and respond to different restart indicators, and

- a processing portion from which calls to `longjmp()` originate.

```c
#include <stdio.h>
#include <setjmp.h>

jmp_buf env;

nested_print(char *buf)
{
    if (buf[0] == '1')
      longjmp(env, 1);
    if (buf[0] == '2')
      longjmp(env, 2);
    printf("%s\n", buf);
}

print(char *buf)
{
    nested_print(buf);
}
```

```
main()
{
    int r, k = 0;
    char buf[BUFSIZ];

    /* perform initialisation */
    printf("setjmp demo\n");

    /* restart location */
    if ((r = setjmp(env)) != 0) {
        if (r == 2)
            exit(0);
        printf("restarted...\n");
    }

    /* processing loop */
    for (;;) {
        printf("%d> ", ++k);
        gets(buf);
        print(buf);
    }
}
```

Listing 10-3: Non-local branches

The processing in function print() might be as deeply nested as possible, as signified by the call to nestedprint(). As long as the caller of setjmp() has not terminated, a call to longjmp() is legitimate from anywhere.

The first character of the string to be printed is used to simulate an exception, and appropriate restart indicators are returned via longjmp(). A restart code of 2 from longjmp() returns 2 to r and thus causes an exit. Any other value will print out the restarting message and proceed back into the processing loop.

10. 5   Non-local Branches from Signal Handlers

It follows that longjmp() might be used from within signal handlers. It is especially useful for signals to interrupt an operation through a non-local branch. This scenario is illustrated with the code fragment in Listing 10-4.

```
#include <stdio.h>
#include <signal.h>
#include <setjmp.h>

jmp_buf env;

void int_handler(int sig)
{
    signal(SIGINT, int_handler);
    longjmp(env, 1);
}

main()
{
    int k = 0;
    char buf[BUFSIZ];

    signal(SIGINT, int_handler);

    if (setjmp(env) != 0)
        printf("restarted...\n");

    for (;;) { /* processing loop */
        printf("%d> ", ++k);
        gets(buf);
        printf("%s\n", buf);
    }
}
```

Listing 10-4: Non-local branch from a signal handler

Processing is simulated by the loop which repeatedly reads and prints a line. As usual, the signal handler is installed by `signal()`, and the context for a restart from processing is prepared by `setjmp()`.

The reader might be tempted to replace the call to `signal()` in `main()` with `sigset()` and remove the same from signal handler `int_handler()` instead. This however does not work.

When the action for a signal X is taken, a process does not respond to further X signals until execution returns from the handler. The delivery of other X signals is said to be *blocked* for the duration of its handler. The processing logic of a handler is simpler with this restriction since it need not consider if a second activation would lead to inconsistencies caused by multiple threads.

Each process has a signal mask which defines the set of signals which are currently blocked. The signal mask is set before calling the handler and cleared before returning. When `longjmp()` is used, the code for returning is skipped and the signal mask is not cleared. As a result, after the first signal is delivered, subsequent signals are blocked. (Note that this signal mask situation is not significant with the use of signal(), as it requires reinstallation of the handler which also clears the signal mask.)

In light of this new concern, two new functions sigsetjmp() and siglongjmp() are introduced.

a. **sigsetjmp() and siglongjmp() library calls** – non-local branches from signal handler

```
#include <setjmp.h>

int sigsetjmp(sigjmp_buf env, int savemask);

void siglongjmp(sigjmp_buf env, int val);
```

The library functions sigsetjmp() and siglongjmp() are similar to setjmp() and longjmp() respectively. However, sigsetjmp() has the additional savemask parameter. If savemask is non-zero, the current signal mask is stored into env at the same time. A subsequent siglongjmp() not only restores the stack contents, but also the signal mask if it was stored with a non-zero savemask.

10. 6   Implementing Timeouts

The approach of non-local jumps from a signal handler may be augmented with an alarm clock. This is a useful method of specifying an upper bound on the period during which a call should block. It might be used to implement timeouts on reading input.

a. alarm() system call – sets alarm clock

```
#include <unistd.h>

unsigned alarm(unsigned sec);
```

The alarm() system call sets the timer to expire after sec real-time seconds has elapsed. When this occurs, the kernel sends the signal SIGALRM to the calling process. There is only one alarm clock per process.

If a second request is issued before the first has expired, alarm() returns the time left before expiration and overwrites that value with the new. If sec is 0, the previous request is cancelled.

The fragment in Listing 10-5 reads input, but is only willing to wait for 20 seconds.

```c
#include <stdio.h>
#include <signal.h>
#include <setjmp.h>

jmp_buf env;

void expire(int buf)
{
    longjmp(env, 1);
}

main()
{
    char buf[BUFSIZ];

    printf("> ");

    if (setjmp(env) != 0) {
        printf("timeout\n");
        exit(1);
    }
    signal(SIGALRM, expire);
    alarm(20);

    gets(buf);
    alarm(0);    /* disable alarm clock since we already have input */
    signal(SIGALRM, SIG_IGN);
    printf("%s\n", buf);
}
```

Listing 10-5: Implementing a timeout period

The code

- anticipates a non-local branch via env,

- installs the SIGALRM handler,

- sets the alarm time appropriately, and

- disables the alarm after use.

When the environment is set as above, the program waits for input from the user. If input is received in time, the alarm is turned off before proceeding with other concerns.

10. 7   Signals and Re-entrant Code

A code fragment is said to be re-entrant if it may be concurrently used by two or more execution threads. Code fragments which manipulate statically allocated storage areas are not re-entrant due to undesirable interaction from the sharing of common data areas amongst active threads.

Fortran subroutines are not re-entrant because they rely on statically allocated local variables and activation records. Since local variables in C and Pascal are allocated at run time, routines which only access local variables are re-entrant.

A number of UNIX library routines are not re-entrant because they write to static variables. These include library routines like `getpwnam()` and `tmpfile()`, because the same library-defined variables are used for every activation. As such variables hold intermediate values and results, the following precautionary measures are important:

- The programmer must ensure that activations of the same non-re-entrant routine do not overlap. By doing so, the intermediate values generated for one activation is not overwritten in another.

- Where the results of an activation of a non-re-entrant routine is required, it must be copied to an appropriate allocation storage location before another call to the routine. This ensures that the result returned by one activation is not overwritten in another.

- Calling non-re-entrant routines from signal handlers should be avoided. This ensures that the condition in (1) would not be breached.

10. 8   Summary

This chapter has discussed the following points:

§   installing of new signal dispositions

```
signal(), sigset()
```

§   non-local branches

```
setjmp(), longjmp(), sigsetjmp(),  siglongjmp()
```

§   setting of an alarm clock timer

```
alarm()
```

§   precautions for re-entrant routines

Detailed information on signals may be found in the `signal(5)` man pages.

10. 9   Exercises

1. Ensure that the appropriate signals are caught by the editor so that the user's editing efforts are not lost by accident.

2. The terminal-locking program cannot function adequately unless it is immuned to signals from the keyboard. Ensure that the appropriate signals are either caught or ignored.

3. Allow the search function of the editor to be prematurely aborted by the SIGINT signal.

4. Consider how the browser responds as it resumes from being suspended. What measures must be taken so that it may continue as though it was not suspended.

11

Handling Terminals

It should be clear at this stage that each terminal line has two independent streams of character flow: input and output. Even if the screen and keyboard are housed in the same unit, the echo of input keystrokes on the screen is not the result of a physical connection between the keyboard and screen circuits.

The initial versions of the browser program actually show that various preprocessing functions occur before an application program gets to read its input. The echoing of keystrokes is not performed by the browser, but by the operating system. The input stream is read by the system driver, and echoed to the output stream to confirm what the user has typed. The later browser version using the *curses* library shows that keyboard echo may be disabled by an application program.

One other observation is that input is typically available to programs on a line basis. An application cannot access an input character until a newline character is encountered. In fact, while characters are buffered in line mode, they can be edited or flushed using the erase-character or kill-line keys. The key bindings of these special functions are also redefinable by the stty command. Similarly, these features may be disabled for situations when each character must be read immediately. Line-editing features are thus not applicable.

This chapter looks at some useful characteristics of terminal lines, the systems software which control them (device driver), and how they may be customised to suit various requirements.

11. 1   Terminal Line Overview

Each terminal line connected to a UNIX machine needs an appropriate device driver for hardware-dependent read and write operations. These device-dependent operations are accessible through the generic operations of the kernel so that reading and writing from devices and files have similar interfaces via file descriptors.

Buffers are incorporated into the device driver so that it may operate asynchronously. A request from a process to the operating system to write a stream of characters may merely transfer data in the output buffer. The process then leaves it to the device driver to physically write it out to the terminal device. A process thus need not always wait for its write operation to complete. Where there is sufficient space in the buffer, both the output process and device driver may proceed independently.

In a similar way, the device driver may also read the terminal line on behalf of a process and transfer data into a buffer. This read-ahead feature is useful so that input characters are not lost, especially when they are typed in before a process is ready to read. Again, where there is sufficient buffer space, both the input process and device driver may proceed independently.

Before the data in the input buffer is made available to programs, or before output data is written to the output buffer, the necessary pre/postprocessing is performed by the terminal line discipline module.

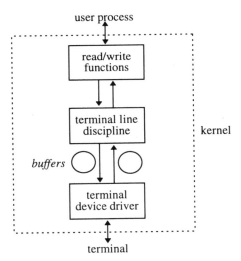

Figure 11-1: Terminal-handling functions

The characteristics of the terminal device are conveniently represented by `termios` structures. This chapter will discuss some of these, and show how they may be examined and modified.

11. 2   Reading and Setting Terminal-device Characteristics

This section merely provides an overview of the characteristics and user customisation possible. Further details are discussed in subsequent sections. From a user point of view, the characteristics of a terminal line may be classified into five logical categories:

- The input modes involve preprocessing of input characters and is implemented by the device driver. The modes specify input characteristics such as whether to strip the eighth bit off input characters, and whether to ignore carriage-return characters or to map carriage-return characters to newline characters instead.

- Similarly, the output modes involve postprocessing of output characters and is also implemented by the device driver. The modes specify output characteristics such as whether to expand tab characters to spaces, whether to slow down to accommodate slow print heads, and whether the newline character should also perform the function of carriage-return character.

- The control modes involve the RS232 serial line characteristics such as the speed of the line, whether parity checking is enabled, and the choice of flow-of-control protocols. Again, these modes are implemented by the device driver.

- The local terminal discipline modes involve local processing and display for feedback purposes. It is implemented by the terminal line discipline module. The modes specify characteristics such as whether to echo input characters, how control characters are displayed, and whether to use line-mode reading with editing facilities. Local modes do not affect the data to be read by a program, but provide useful input features.

- The special character mappings specify the key mappings for functions such as backspacing, sending signals (such as interrupt, suspend or quit), and indicating an end-of-file condition. As the key and terminal emulation mappings are customisable by the user, this feature has often confused UNIX novices.

The characteristics, as listed above, may be obtained and modified via the library calls `tcgetattr()` and `tcsetattr()`. While a more general terminal interface is available via system `ioctl` (input/output control) calls, `tcgetattr()` and `tcsetattr()` provide similar functionality and is the preferred and simpler interface.

a. `tcgetattr()` and `tcsetattr()` library calls – general terminal interface

```
#include <termios.h>

int tcgetattr(int fildes, struct termios *termios_p);
int tcsetattr(int fildes, int optional_actions,
                         struct termios *termios_p);
```

The `tcgetattr()` library call retrieves the terminal attributes associated with the file descriptor `fildes` into the `termios` structure referenced by `termios_p`. The complementary `tcputattr()` library call sets the terminal attributes associated with the file descriptor `fildes` according to the characteristics represented by the `termios` structure referenced by `termios_p`.

The `termios` structure used to represent the device characteristics has five fields, and these correspond to the five logical groups mentioned earlier.

```
struct termios {
    tcflag_t c_iflag;     /* input modes   */
    tcflag_t c_oflag;     /* output modes  */
    tcflag_t c_cflag;     /* control modes */
    tcflag_t c_lflag;     /* local modes   */
    cc_t  c_cc[NCCS];     /* control chars */
};
```

`tcgetattr()` and `tcsetattr()` return 0 to indicate success, and –1 to indicate failure.

The additional parameter `optional_actions` for `tcsetattr()` specifies when the new settings should take effect. Recognised values are enumerated in Table 11-1.

`optional_actions` parameter	Semantics
TCSANOW	The change indicated by *`termios_p` occurs immediately.
TCSADRAIN	The change occurs after all output written to `fildes` has been transmitted.
TCSAFLUSH	The change occurs after all output written to `fildes` has been transmitted. In addition, all input that has been received but is not yet read is discarded.

Table 11-1: Semantics of `optional_action` *parameter*

11. 3 Interpreting and Operating on `termios` Fields

A terminal characteristic may be represented as

- a flag,
- a mask, or
- a value

in the `termios` structure. In this section, we review how these might be accessed and modified.

a. Terminal characteristic represented by a flag

A terminal device characteristic which is either enabled or disabled is called a flag. It is easily represented by a single bit in a `termios` field, and might control whether canonical mode processing (reading in line-mode with editing facilities) is enabled or disabled, or whether keystrokes are to be echoed to the screen.

An associated bit offset for each characteristic dictates that each flag be associated with an appropriate bit pattern given by the expression `1<<(offset-1)`. For example, a characteristic which is denoted by the ninth bit (from the right) may be operated upon via the pattern mask `000400` (octal). This pattern mask is used to mask over the appropriate `struct termios` field to turn the feature either on or off.

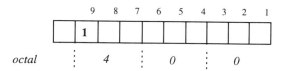

Figure 11-2: Determining a pattern-mask value

For example, reading in canonical mode is defined by the second bit (from the right) of the local processing mode field `c_lflag` (*l* for local processing). The symbol `ICANON` is assigned the equivalent pattern `000002` in the `termios.h` header file. Canonical-mode processing is determined and modified by the code fragment in Listing 11-1.

```
#include <termios.h>

main()
{
    struct termios term;

    if (tcgetattr(STDIN_FILENO, &term) < 0)
        report_err("tcgetattr()");
    printf("Canonical mode is %s\n",
```

```
                (term.c_lflag & ICANON ? "on" : "off"));

        if (make_canon_mode)
            term.c_lflag |= ICANON;
        else
            term.c_lflag &= ~ICANON;
        if (tcsetattr(STDIN_FILENO, TCSANOW, &term) < 0)
            report_err("tcsetattr()");
        exit(0);
    }
```

Listing 11-1: Manipulating bit characteristic in termios *structure*

The summary of bitwise operations in Table 11-2 are standard means of manipulating single bits.

Code	Operation	Remarks
field & pattern	access the flag: zero result indicates that flag is disabled	The result is determined by the single 1 bit in the mask pattern since the rest are masked out by bit 0s.
field |= pattern	flag is enabled	field remains unchanged, except for an extra bit 1 in pattern.
field &= ~pattern	flag is disabled	field remains unchanged, except for the bit 0 in ~pattern.

Table 11-2: Bit operations for a flag

b. Terminal characteristic represented by a mask

A terminal device characteristic which has more than two options cannot be represented by a single bit, but by multiple bits called a mask. A mask is operated upon in about the same way as a flag. Each option has a corresponding bit pattern at the appropriate bit offset. However, in addition, a general mask pattern is required to indicate the significant bits in the struct termios field pertaining to the characteristic.

A characteristic represented by a mask is accessed by clearing insignificant bit patterns from the corresponding struct termios field. This is the use of the general mask pattern. Similarly, an option is set by first clearing the existing value with the complement of the general mask pattern, and then masking the specific mask pattern for the particular option.

For example, an RS232 line may be set to transmit and receive character sizes of five, six, seven or eight bits. This is indicated by the fifth and sixth bits (from the right) of the control mode field c_cflag (*c* for control) as shown in Figure 11-3.

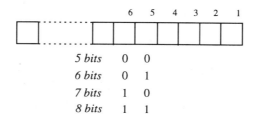

| | 6 | 5 | 4 | 3 | 2 | 1 |

5 bits	0 0
6 bits	0 1
7 bits	1 0
8 bits	1 1

Figure 11-3: Determining specific mask values

The general mask pattern CSIZE is derived from the significance of the fifth and sixth bits in the field. This gives the value of 060. Similarly, the specific mask patterns for character-sizes five, six, seven and eight are 000, 020, 040 and 060 respectively. The symbols CS5, CS6, CS7 and CS8 are assigned these corresponding values. The code fragment in Listing 11-2 reads and sets this terminal line characteristic. Note how the general pattern mask is always used to mask out unrelated bits before testing against or assigning the specific masks:

```
#include <termios.h>

main()
{
    struct termios term;
    int size;

    if (tcgetattr(STDIN_FILENO, &term) < 0)
        report_err("tcgetattr");
    size = term.c_cflag & CSIZE;
    if (size == CS8)
        printf("using 8 bits/byte\n");
    else
        printf("using less than 8 bits/byte\n");

    /* set to 7 bits/byte */
    term.c_cflag &= ~CSIZE;
    term.c_cflag |= CS7;
    if (tcsetattr(STDIN_FILENO, TCSANOW, &term) < 0)
        report_err("tcsetattr");
    exit(0);
}
```

Listing 11-2: Manipulating mask characteristic in termios *structure*

The summary of bitwise operations in Table 11-3 are the standard means of manipulating masks.

Code	Operation	Remarks
`field & gen_mask`	access mask value	The result is determined by the significant bits as indicated in the general mask pattern `gen_mask`.
`field &= ~gen_mask;` `field | = spe_mask;`	mask is set with new value	`field` remains unchanged except for bits which are cleared by `gen_mask` and given new values via the specific mask pattern `spe_mask`.

Table 11-3: Bit operations for a mask

c. Terminal characteristic represented by a value

Bit or mask patterns are however not suitable for a terminal characteristic which uses a value to indicate key bindings. There are just too many of these characteristics to be recorded in a word. Furthermore, it is more efficient to align values on byte boundaries. The strategy adopted is to record key-binding values in a byte array with predefined subscripts.

The key-binding values are stored in array c_cc of the termios structure. Predefined subscripts are defined in the associated termios.h file. For example, the subscript for the interrupt key is VINTR. It is used to index array c_cc when accessing or redefining its binding. The code fragment in Listing 11-3 prints the current binding, and defines ^K to send an interrupt signal instead.

```
#include <termios.h>

main()
{
    struct termios term;

    if (tcgetattr(STDIN_FILENO, &term) < 0)
        report_err("tcgetattr");
    printf("Interrupt key is '\\%o'\n", term.c_cc[VINTR]);

    /* set ^K to generate interrupt signal */
    term.c_cc[VINTR] = 'K' & 037;
    if (tcsetattr(STDIN_FILENO, TCSANOW, &term) < 0)
        report_err("tcsetattr");
    exit(0);
}
```

Listing 11-3: Manipulating key bindings of terminal

In this section, we discussed how terminal characteristics, whether represented as flags, masks or values, may be queried and modified. The following sections provide details of terminal characteristics that are customisable.

11. 4   Key Bindings for Special Characters

The special-character key bindings for various terminal line discipline local-mode functions and generating signals to foreground processes may be queried and modified. Users typically define key bindings for various functions according to their personal preferences and similarities with other systems that they might have used. The `stty` command is implemented using an equivalent terminal interface.

Key bindings are often useful in interactive applications. While adopting non-canonical mode input, an application may continue to adopt the same key map as that for canonical mode. Such a design decision possibly makes the application more acceptable to the user. This could increase the likelihood of success.

An example of this situation is the browser/editor implementation using `cbreak()` mode with the *curses* library. It would be useful for the erase character function to dynamically adopt the current key bindings as set by the `stty` command. So, if a user prefers, say, the ^A for a backspace, ^A should also be the application's backspace command key.

The remainder of this section provides a brief description of each special character, the symbolic subscript to access the array `c_cc`, and defaults which are typically used.

The signals `SIGINT`, `SIGQUIT` and `SIGTSTP` (as discussed in the previous chapter) are sent to foreground processes attached to the terminal when appropriate key bindings for `VINTR`, `VQUIT`, `VSUSP` are typed at the terminal. Background processes and processes belonging to a different login by the same user will not be affected. The key binding for `VDSUSP` also sends a `SIGTSTP` signal, but only when the key is read rather than when it is typed, as in the case for `VSUSP`.

Description	Subscript	Likely default	Enabled by
interrupt signal (`SIGINT`)	VINTR	^C	`ISIG` in `c_lflag`
quit signal (`SIGQUIT`)	VQUIT	^\	`ISIG` in `c_lflag`
suspend signal (`SIGTSTP`)	VSUSP	^Z	`ISIG` in `c_lflag`
delayed suspend (`SIGTSTP`)	VDSUSP	^Y	`ISIG` in `c_lflag`

Table 11-4: Special key bindings

This functionality is only applicable if the ISIG option (see local-mode options) is enabled. Getting the device driver to send such signals (especially SIGINT) is convenient. Without this feature, users will need to login again at another terminal to interrupt a foreground process.

When reading in line mode (that is, ICANON option is enabled – see local mode options), the local-mode functions, as in the following table, provide some assistance in terms of line editing.

erase previous character	VERASE	^H	ICANON in c_lflag
erase line	VKILL	^U	ICANON in c_lflag
end-of-file indicator	VEOF	^D	ICANON in c_lflag

The key bindings in the following table supplements the local-mode functions described already, and are available when the IEXTEN option (see local-mode options) is enabled:

erase previous word	VWERASE	^W	IEXTEN in c_lflag
discard (flush) output	VDISCARD	^O	IEXTEN in c_lflag
reprint all input	VREPRINT	^R	IEXTEN in c_lflag
literal next	VLNEXT	^V	IEXTEN in c_lflag

The reprint option is useful if the contents of the line buffer are not properly reflected. This could be due to the screen being messed up by a write command message from another user. Since the terminal driver attaches special meanings to various keys, these may only be read as input if such keys are prefixed by the literal key.

If the IXON option (see local-mode options) is enabled, output may be temporarily stopped with the key binding for VSTOP, and continued with VSTART.

stop output	VSTOP	^S	IXON in c_iflag
start output	VSTART	^Q	IXON in c_iflag

VMIN and VTIME are not special characters, but are instead attributes used in non-canonical mode processing. They are mentioned here because their attribute values are also represented in the c_cc array. Their usage would be discussed in a subsequent section.

Minimum characters before read returns	VMIN	1	~ICANON in c_lflag
Time to wait before read returns	VTIME	0	~ICANON in c_lflag

Because VMIN and VTIME are used in non-canonical mode, they might (in some implementations) share array slots with the other canonical-mode attributes described above. It is thus advisable that for non-canonical processing, an extra `termios` structure be used so that the original value is preserved for resetting terminal characteristics back to canonical mode.

11. 5 Local Modes

The `c_lflag` field of the `termios` structure is used to represent the characteristics of local terminal functions.

We encountered the first three local modes when we discussed the binding of special characters in the previous section. Since the various signals are sent in response to the respective bound keys, those keys will never be read in by the program, unless the ISIG mode is off.

ISIG
: If set, the input stream is checked against the special characters for signals, and a corresponding SIGINT, SIGQUIT or SIGTSTP signal is sent to the foreground processes.

ICANON
: If set, canonical-mode input processing makes input available on a line-by-line basis (as delimited by a line-feed character). Line-mode reading allows for erase and kill editing. If not set, reading depends on the VTIME and VMIN parameters, to be described separately.

IEXTEN
: If set, the special characters for VWERASE, VREPRINT, VDISCARD, and VLNEXT are added to the canonical input processing above. In addition, the local flags TOSTOP, ECHOCTL, ECHOPRT, ECHOKE, FLUSHO, and PENDIN have their intended effect.

As mentioned earlier, the echo of keyboard input is performed by the terminal line discipline module. This is enabled by the ECHO flag, but the following flags specify how the echo of erase, kill and control characters are carried out. The ECHOPRT and ECHOK modes do not normally apply to CRT terminals but to typewriter-style terminals where a hard-copy log is useful.

ECHO
: If set, characters in the input stream are echoed to the output stream.

ECHOE
: If set, and ECHO is set, the erase character is echoed as ASCII characters backspace (BS) space (SP) backspace (BS). This is what most users are accustomed to.

ECHOPRT
: If set, and ECHO is set, and ECHOE is not set, the erase character is echoed as the character that is being erased.

ECHOKE
: If set, and ECHO is set, the kill character is echoed with the style used for ECHOE or ECHOPRT for the entire line killed.

ECHOK
: If set, and ECHO is set, and ECHOKE is not set, newline (NL) is echoed after the kill character.

ECHOCTL   If set, control characters are echoed as ^x, and the delete (DEL) character is
                    echoed as ^?.

The FLUSHO flag implements a time and resource-saving feature: time and effort need not be
spent writing the buffer to the terminal, if its contents are to be ignored anyway. However,
output might still not terminate immediately for certain installations where additional buffers in
terminal servers or terminal emulators exist.

The PENDIN flag augments the feedback given by the ECHO flag. It applies when there
is more input than required: For example, when more than one line is already typed in
canonical-input mode, it is useful to provide feedback as to the contents of the buffer before
reading the second line.

FLUSHO   If set, output is flushed by the VDISCRD character.

NOFLSH   The input and output buffers are flushed after generating interrupt, suspend
                    or quit signals. If set, the buffers are not flushed.

PENDIN   If set, characters in the buffer (pending input at next read operation) are re-
                    echoed.

11.6   Input Modes

The c_iflag field of the termios structure specifies the basic terminal input mode.

The IGNBRK and BRKINT options describe how the break key on a keyboard is handled.

IGNBRK   If set, the break condition generated by the terminal is ignored.

BRKINT   If set, and IGNBRK is not set, a break condition flushes input and output, and
                    sends SIGINT. If not set, and IGNBRK is also not set, the condition is read
                    as a null character.

The IGNPAR and PARMRK options describe how parity errors are handled.

IGNPAR   If set, characters with parity errors are ignored.

PARMRK   If set, and IGNPAR is not set, parity errors are read as character sequence
                    '\0' '\377' x, where x is the error byte. If neither PARMRK or IGNPAR is set,
                    a parity error is read as '\0'.

The IUCLC, INLCR, IGNCR and ICRNL options perform limited character set mapping. The first allows for case insensitivity, while the other options allow for the carriage-return key to double up as a newline key, or for both to be swapped.

IUCLC	If set, upper-case alphabetic characters are translated into the corresponding lower-case characters.
INLCR	If set, a NL character is translated to CR.
IGNCR	If set, a CR character is ignored.
ICRNL	If set, a CR character is translated to NL.

The IXON and IXANY options specify XON/XOFF flow control, and how to continue output to the terminal after a STOP request.

IXON	If set, the VSTOP and VSTART characters allow for XON/XOFF flow control to restart output.
IXANY	If set, any character is used in XON/XOFF flow control to restart output.

The IMAXBEL option specifies the feedback and possible action for long input lines.

IXOFF	If set and IXON is set, the STOP character is used to stop input when the buffer is almost full.
IMAXBEL	If set, the BEL character is echoed if the input line is too long. Further input is not stored, and existing characters are not flushed. If not set, BEL is not echoed and the input line is flushed.

11. 7   Output Modes

The c_oflag field of the termios structure specifies the basic terminal output mode.

OPOST	If set, output is postprocessed, as indicated by flags which follow.

The options below perform output character mapping to suit the particular output device.

OLCUC	If set, lower-case alphabetic characters are translated into the corresponding upper-case characters.
ONLCR	If set, a NL character is translated to a CR-NL sequence on output.
OCRNL	If set, a CR character is translated to NL on output.
ONOCR	If set, a CR character is not printed at column 0.
ONLRET	If set, a NL performs a CR function.

Older terminals (especially typewriter-types with mechanical parts) cannot function with high baud rates and might require the output to be slow for certain actions like carriage return. Often, a fixed time-delay is not necessary, merely a filler (non-printable) character.

OFILL   If set, use filler characters for delay instead of a time-delay.

OFDEL   If set, the DEL character is used as the filler character, or else the null character is used.

11. 8   Hardware Control Modes

The c_cflag field of the termios structure specifies the hardware control of the terminal. The characteristics include standard parameters like the baud rate, data bits, stop bits and parity. As discussed earlier, characteristics with multiple options require a general mask pattern.

CBAUD   Baud-rate general mask.

B0   The connection is terminated.

B50, ... B38400   50, 75, 110, 134, 150, 200, 300, 600, 1200, 1800, 2400, 4800, 9600, 19200, 38400 pattern masks.

CSIZE   Character-size general mask.

CS5, CS6, CS7,   5, 6, 7, 8 bits/byte pattern masks.
CS8

CSTOPB   If set, use two stop bits; else, one.

PARENB   If set, even-parity generation and detection is enabled.

PARODD   If set, odd-parity instead of even is enabled.

PAREXT   Extended parity for mark and space parity.

HUPCL   If set, the line is disconnected when the last process with the line terminates.

CLOCAL   If set, a local line (not a modem) is assumed.

11. 9   Using Non-Canonical Input Mode

Non-canonical-mode input depends on the two parameters MIN and TIME. How they are assigned new values has been described. MIN represents the minimum number of input characters that should be available before the characters are returned to the user. TIME is a timer of 0.10 second granularity that is used to timeout data transmissions. The four possible values for MIN and TIME are summarised below.

mode 1:
MIN>0, TIME>0

In this case, TIME serves as an intercharacter timer and is activated after the first character is received. Since it is an intercharacter timer, it is reset after a character is received. The read is satisfied if MIN characters are received, or if the timer expires. The characters received to that point are then returned to the user. Note that if TIME expires, at least one character will be returned because the timer would not have been enabled unless a character has been read.

mode 2:
MIN>0, TIME=0

In this case, since the value of TIME is zero, the timer plays no role and only MIN is significant. A pending read is not satisfied until MIN characters are received.

mode 3:
MIN=0, TIME>0

In this case, where MIN=0, TIME no longer represents an intercharacter timer. Instead, it serves as a read timer that is activated as soon as a read is requested. A read is satisfied when a single character is received, or the read timer expires in TIME*0.1 seconds, in which case, no character is returned.

mode 4:
MIN=0, TIME=0

In this case, return is immediate. Without waiting for more characters in the stream, the minimum of either the number of characters requested or the number of characters currently available, is returned.

Non-canonical input will be better understood by analysing the following short program in Listing 11-4.

```
#include <stdio.h>
#include <unistd.h>
#include <termios.h>

main()
{
    char c;
    struct termios term;

    if (tcgetattr(STDIN_FILENO, &term) < 0)        /* read term modes */
        report_err("tcgetattr");
    term.c_lflag &= ~ICANON;                   /* turn off canonical mode */
    if (tcsetattr(STDIN_FILENO, TCSANOW, &term)< 0)/* set term modes */
        report_err("tcsetattr");
```

```
    while ((c = getchar()) != '\004')
        putchar(c);

    term.c_lflag |= ICANON;                    /* turn on canonical mode */
    if (tcsetattr(STDIN_FILENO, TCSANOW, &term)< 0)/* set term modes */
        report_err("tcsetattr");
    exit(0);
}
```

Listing 11-4: Reading in non-canonical mode

The program first turns canonical input mode off, reads and prints characters until it encounters ^D, and then turns canonical input mode on again. Compiling and running this program might produce output as shown, where output is interspersed by groups of four characters:

```
$ gcc -o read1 read1.c
$ ./read1
abcdabcdefghefghijk
ijk
```

This occurs because we did not set the appropriate values for TIME and MIN, and they had residual values 0 and 4 respectively[1]. This behaviour corresponds to mode 2 in the classification at the beginning of this section. In most situations of reading in non-canonical mode, local echo would be turned off, and each character is read immediately as it is entered. As illustrated in Listing 11-5, this situation is met with TIME=0 and MIN=1.

```
#include <stdio.h>
#include <unistd.h>
#include <termios.h>

main()
{
    char c;
    struct termios term;

    if (tcgetattr(STDIN_FILENO, &term) < 0)        /* read term modes */
        report_err("tcgetattr");
    term.c_lflag &= ~ICANON;                  /* turn off canonical mode */
    term.c_lflag &= ~ECHO;                    /* turn off echo mode */
```

---

[1] On inspecting /usr/include/sys/termios.h, you will discover that the TIME and MIN elements share the same position with the EOL and EOF characters respectively. The EOL character is an additional line-delimiter character and is typically left undefined (i.e. 0), while the EOF character is typically ^D (i.e. ASCII value 4).

```
        term.c_cc[VTIME] = 0;                               /* set TIME to 0 */
        term.c_cc[VMIN] = 1;                                /* set MIN to 1 */
        if (tcsetattr(STDIN_FILENO, TCSANOW, &term)< 0)/* set term modes */
            report_err("tcsetattr");

        while ((c = getchar()) != '\004')
            putchar(c);

        term.c_lflag |= ICANON;                 /* turn on canonical mode */
        term.c_lflag |= ECHO;                       /* turn on echo mode */
        if (tcsetattr(STDIN_FILENO, TCSANOW, &term)< 0)/* set term modes */
            report_err("tcsetattr");
        exit(0);
}
```

Listing 11-5: Setting TIME and MIN for non-canonical mode

The second version in Listing 11-5 gives the results that we expect for an interactive program whose keys are read as they are pressed, and the program may choose whether to echo the input.

However, the key binding of the EOF condition is changed when we revert to canonical input mode. This problem is easily corrected by using two termios structures, as seen in Listing 11-6. The first termios structure stores the original mode and is used to restore terminal settings to the original modes, while the second is used to store the current terminal mode used by the program.

```
#include <stdio.h>
#include <unistd.h>
#include <termios.h>

main()
{
    char c;
    struct termios origin, term;

    if (tcgetattr(STDIN_FILENO, &term) < 0)        /* read term modes */
        report_err("tcgetattr");
    origin = term;
    term.c_lflag &= ~ICANON;                    /* turn off canonical mode */
    term.c_lflag &= ~ECHO;                          /* turn off echo mode */
    term.c_cc[VTIME] = 0;                           /* set TIME to 0 */
    term.c_cc[VMIN] = 1;                            /* set MIN to 1 */
    if (tcsetattr(STDIN_FILENO, TCSANOW, &term)< 0)/* set term modes */
        report_err("tcsetattr");

    while ((c = getchar()) != '\004')
        putchar(c);

    if (tcsetattr(STDIN_FILENO, TCSANOW, &origin)< 0)/* origin modes */
```

```
        report_err("tcsetattr");
    exit(0);
}
```

Listing 11-6: Setting and restoring TIME and MIN

a. Non-blocking read operations

The case where both TIME and MIN are 0 results in non-blocking read operations. Here, getchar() returns -1 to indicate that no key has been pressed and thus, nothing has been read.

```
for (;;) {
    while ((c = getchar()) == -1)
        /* do other things since input is not yet available */;
    if (c == '\004')
        break;
    else
        putchar(c);
}
```

Alternatively, the read() and write() system calls may also be used instead of getchar() and putchar(). Here, the former returns 0 if no character has been read.

```
for (;;) {
    while (read(STDIN_FILENO, &c, 1) == 0)
        /* do other things since input is not yet available */;
    if (c == '\004')
        break;
    else
        write(STDOUT_FILENO, &c, 1);
}
```

Unless necessary, we should avoid using non-blocking read operations, as the overhead for such polling is high because busy-waiting is employed. There are two possible alternatives:

- In the example above, there is no necessity to use canonical mode 4. Canonical mode 2, with MIN=1, would have been sufficient. In this case, the process is suspended until input is available.

- The use of canonical mode 3 would provide more time to wait for input. This reduces the busy-waiting overhead. The value of the TIME parameter would depend on computation requirements between two read requests.

11. 10   Summary

This chapter has provided an insight into the terminal device model in UNIX. The following points were discussed:

§   device characteristics and `termios` structure

   `tcgetattr(), tcsetattr()`

§   input modes, output modes, control modes, local modes, special character binding

§   non-canonical-mode reading

While the *curses* library calls could be sufficient for screen display and typical keyboard input, `termios` calls are useful for improving the consistency of key bindings. The features discussed will also be useful when implementing a communications system over a serial line.

   Additional reference material may be found in the `stty(1)`, `termios(7)` and `termio(7)` man pages. Pseudo ttys are used for network access. More information on this facility is found in the `pts(7)` man page.

11. 11   Exercises

1. Improve the key bindings of the browser so that it also recognises the bindings used in canonical input mode.

2. Implement an `echo` program so that the output of a program may be concurrently displayed on another terminal.

Appendix

UNIX Programming Tools

In this appendix, we examine some of the program development tools available in the UNIX environment. Standard programs such as the compiler and editor are tools too. We will attempt to make better use of these and others found in standard UNIX releases.

A. 1 `vi` for File Editing and More

Familiarity of the `vi` editing model and command structure is very important because it allows for quick and effective navigation as well as choice of precise edit operators. For example, a move-to-next-paragraph via `}`, is more effective than moving down a line n times to the same location. Similarly, delete-word via **dw**, is more effective than deleting a character m times. The `vi(1) man` page contains a quick `vi` summary.

`vi` features which specifically help with the modification of program sources are highlighted in the remainder of this section. Since `vi` reads the initialisation file `.exrc` at startup, settings which are applicable to a project may be included in the appropriate directory.

a. Key mapping

The `map` facility in `vi` allows a key to be mapped to a key sequence. Preparing such sequences appropriately reduces typing effort during program modification. It is beneficial to use a comment template since comments are necessary and expected in programs. Similarly, templates for large program constructs (e.g. function definitions) will also be useful.

A comment template might be formed by inserting the standard comment delimiters with two carriage-return characters in between. The keystrokes to achieve it in vi might be bound to ^T (for comment template) via the command

```
:map ^T i/*^M^M*/^[
```

where ^T, ^M and ^[represent the control-T, control-M and Escape characters respectively (appropriately prefixed with the literal key). Appropriate templates for C constructs, such as a function definition, might be implemented using the same method.

In addition, the symbol sequence #n might be used to denote the function key. Thus, the following command sequence maps the F1 key to provide a function template:

```
:map #1 ix()^M{^M}^M^[
```

Templates defined by map commands might also be placed in the startup file, so that they need not be rekeyed for each vi session.

b. Match option

The vi command % shows each matching braces {}, brackets [] and parentheses () in the interactive mode. When the showmatch option is enabled, matching delimiters are also matched in input mode. This is useful for confirming the nesting of complex expressions during program entry.

```
:set showmatch
```

c. Setting tab stop

Tab characters, rather than fixed spaces, are conveniently used to introduce an indent level for a new construct. However, by default, they expand at eight-column intervals. A deeply nested program would likely require the horizontal space which an 80-column terminal screen cannot offer. A solution here is to reduce tab intervals:

```
:set tabstop=4
```

d. Setting shift width

The vi key commands > and < for shifting program fragments to the right and left are useful for shifting constructs whose indentation levels might have changed. The width of each shift is governed by the shiftwidth option. For this purpose, it would be convenient for the value of shiftwidth to correspond with that for tabstop.

        :set shiftwidth=4

e. Autoindent Option

When enabled, the autoindent option inserts appropriate white spaces to reflect the structure of programs.

        :set autoindent

At the end of a construct, the complementary ^d command is used to backtab to the previous indentation level. By default, a deindent is also an eight-column shift. But this may be modified by redefining the value of shiftwidth.

f. Line-number option

Since UNIX compilers report program errors with respect to the line number, a quick method to position the cursor at a particular line is useful. The vi already provides a command to locate the cursor at line **n** via the command **n G**. However, on-screen line numbering is useful for locating neighbouring lines. When enabled, the number option prefixes the display of each line with the line number.

        :set number

Note that line numbers produced using this option are merely displayed on the editing screen, and not stored in the file.

g. Using tags

It is often difficult to remember the location of various definitions when a large program is spread over many source files. vi solves this problem by allowing the user to construct a map between symbolic names and particular locations in named files.

Such a map is known as a tags file. Each line in the tags file contains a single tag association:

```
symbolic-name   file   navigation-command
```

Typically, `symbolic-name` would be the name of a program entity such as a function or type definition. `file` is the name of the file `vi` will open, and `navigation-command` is the associated `vi` command which is to be executed to locate the cursor appropriately. Typically, this involves searching for the appropriate definition, but need not be limited to this.

The tags command in turn looks up a symbolic name, opens the associated file and locates the cursor at the specific position.

```
:ta name
```

Fortunately, the process of constructing the tags file might be automated by using the `ctags` program. It is consistent with the UNIX tools philosophy: whatever may be automated, should be. Furthermore, the information in a tags file changes periodically as programs are modified. `ctags` is described in the next section.

A. 2   **ctags** for Generating C Tags File

While the tags description file for `vi` may be constructed manually, the `ctags` program automates this procedure for C programs. The simplest method is to invoke `ctags` on all `.c` files (assuming that all `.c` files in the directory are relevant):

```
$ ctags *.c
```

By default, the `ctags` program constructs tag descriptions for function definitions in files specified in the command line. With the `-t` option, tag descriptions are also included for `typedefs`. Output is directed to the file named `tags`. This is the name which `vi` would accept without requiring additional customisation. The output file may also be specified via the `-f` *filename* flag.

The output of `ctags` may be appended to an existing tags description file if the `-a` option is specified. In addition, an update is specified via the `-u` flag. In this case, `ctags` first deletes existing tags descriptions for the specified files before inserting the updated entries. The alternative method of deleting the tags description file and reinvoking `ctags` is usually more efficient. Revising the tags description file is however necessary during the process of program development when functions are added and/or deleted or moved to a different program file.

If ctags is used for files in more than one directory, then the full pathname must be included. The following commands show two possibilities:

```
$ ctags `find . -name '*.c' -print`
$ find . -name '*.c' -exec ctags -u {} \;
```

Lastly, equivalent tags generators for other languages may also be built.

A. 3 The gcc Compiler

Most compilers on UNIX perform the tasks of compiling and linking, as mentioned previously. Like many other compiler shells in the UNIX environment, gcc is really a facilitator program which executes appropriate programs to complete the task given. For example, gcc typically calls the processor cpp, the C compiler cc1 (or the C++ compiler cc1plus, depending on the context), the assembler as, as well as the loader ld.

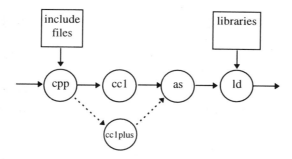

Figure A-1: gcc overview

Command-line options are interpreted by gcc for the purpose of either deciding which other programs are to be executed, or passing the options on to those programs. We have seen that the -c option prevents loading and leaves the output as that produced by the assembler. Other similar options stop after preprocessing (-E option) or compiling (-S option). This provides the flexibility of performing non-standard translations.

The -x option allows the input language to be stated explicitly: -x c, -x c++ or -x objective-c.

Options which are handed to the preprocessor include -I, -D and -U. The -I option provides an alternative path to finding #include files. The -Dmacro=defn option defines preprocessor symbols. If only -Dname is given, the macro *name* is defined as "1". The definition method is preferred over the #define method if the definition is frequently changed, like the DEBUG flag we saw earlier on. The -U option is the converse of the -D and it undefines a predefined macro.

Useful flags for the compiler proper are -O, -g and -p. The -O option turns on the optimisation mode. This increases compilation time and memory resources for the analysis of larger functions, but should improve run-time performance. The -O2 option allows for even more optimisation possibilities.

An effect of optimisation is that the order of code execution might not proceed as expected from reading the original source code. This is because the code generator reorders code to improve register usage as well as to avoid re-evaluation of values which might already be known. This might make debugging traces difficult to follow.

The -g generates code to be used with the debugger gdb. Generally, there is a wide disparity between high-level language mechanisms and the generated machine codes which implement them. Relying on machine code for source-level debugging is difficult. Appropriate source-level information must therefore be embedded in the generated code. This information is however not always necessary for the sole purpose of execution.

As an example, variable names are converted to addresses in the data segment during compilation since this is how variables are implemented. Program execution does not require that the original name be retained. However, for the purpose of relating locations to names, it is necessary that some form of the compile-time symbol table be used during debugging.

The -g option instructs the compiler to retain sufficient source information for run time. Debugging may then proceed nearer to the source-program level than remaining at the level of the generated machine code.

The -p and -pg options generate code to produce execution profiles. The profilers prof and gprof read and interpret the profile information for each run accordingly. They provide information on the dynamic characteristics of a particular execution of the program. The debugger gdb and the profilers prof and gprof will be elaborated on in subsequent sections.

Options which gcc passes on to the linker include -o, -l and -L. The -l option specifies a library to be used during linking by ld. We have seen the inclusion of the *curses* library via -lcurses. In general, specifying -lname causes the library /usr/lib/libname.a to be used in resolving external symbols. In this case, /usr/lib/libcurses.a is used.

The -L option specifies additional library search paths to be used prior to searching predefined paths, such as /usr/lib. This is useful for user-implemented libraries (since system libraries are already placed in predefined locations).

Finally, the -o option specifies the name for the executable file in place of the default a.out.

A. 4 make to Make Up-to-date Versions

The make program is often an indispensable tool in the development of non-trivial programs built from multiple source files. It reads a dependency specification file, and proceeds to build a specified target based on the dependency information. This is best illustrated with an example.

Suppose an application consists of three source files x.c, y.c and z.c, and two other interface files def.h and x.h. Suppose further that the source files require the interface files as illustrated:

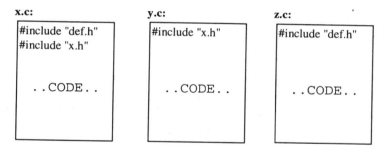

Figure A-2: Sample program structure

The source file x.c is dependent on both def.h and x.h, y.c on x.h, and z.c on def.h. This dependency implies that if ever x.h is modified, both x.c and y.c must be recompiled. In general, a source file must be recompiled if its dependent files have been modified, although make can be applied to other types of processing besides compilation. The procedure to produce a target must be repeated if the source or dependents have been modified (thus making the target out of date).

The Makefile dependency specification for the make command might contain the following lines:

```
x.o: def.h x.h
y.o: x.h
z.o: def.h
prog: x.o y.o z.o
<tab>    gcc -o prog x.o y.o z.o -lcurses -ltermcap
```

Each line with the colon symbol (:) specifies the dependencies of a target. The components on the left side is the target, while those on the right side specify the components on which the target depends.

The line after a dependency specification which begins with a tab character specifies how the target of the dependency specification is to be constructed.

The above does not look complete. While the shell command line to construct prog is specified, how the .o files are to be produced has not been specified. This is usually dependent on rules which are predefined on a system-wide basis. (However, since we are using gcc, the system-wide definitions might not work appropriately.) A quick and simple fix adds the following commands:

```
x.o: def.h x.h
<tab>     gcc -c x.c
y.o: x.h .
<tab>     gcc -c y.c
z.o: def.h
<tab>     gcc -c z.c
```

make is invoked to construct the target prog via the command make prog. It performs a dependency analysis based on the specifications in the Makefile. It then walks the dependency graph *recursively*: prog may be constructed by linking the three object files x.o, y.o and z.o. If these are not up to date (not compiled since the sources they depend upon were modified), they must be built according to the associated rules.

Eventually, make deduces that the following four commands must be invoked by:

```
gcc -c x.c
gcc -c y.c
gcc -c z.c
gcc -o prog x.o y.o z.o -lcurses
```

However, specifying how each .c source file must be compiled is often tedious. make allows for general rules to perform such conversions. The predefined means for transforming .c files to .o object files is by using the standard C compiler cc. This is specified in system-wide initialisation files as:

```
CC = cc
.c.o:
<tab>     $(CC) $(CFLAGS) $(CPPFLAGS) -c $<
```

While this make specification looks cryptic, it may be interpreted as follows:

- This specification is known as a *suffix rule*. Such a rule provides the means (a shell command line) to transform all .c to .o files. In effect, it specifies how C programs might be compiled.

- The dollar $ character is not a literal character for the shell command. When used with parentheses, as with $(CFLAGS), it substitutes the value of the named macro. By default, the CC macro is defined to be cc, while CFLAGS and CPPFLAGS are typically left undefined. Requesting the value of an undefined macro in make returns the empty string.

- $< is a macro that returns the name of a dependency file used with the rule. In this case, it would be the name of the .c file from which we are to derive the .o file.

There are now two alternatives to the "tedious" approach mentioned earlier. Firstly, we could redefine the .c.o suffix rule by including a new rule in our Makefile specification:

```
.c.o:
<tab>    gcc -c $<
```

However, as the original suffix rule will show, it is usually more flexible to use macro definitions in Makefile specifications. Since it uses the CC macro for the name of the compiler, the second fix is merely to redefine CC to gcc. Thus, a suitable Makefile is:

```
CC = gcc
x.o: def.h x.h
y.o: x.h
z.o: def.h
prog: x.o y.o z.o
<tab>    $(CC) -o prog x.o y.o z.o -lcurses
```

While the target prog to be built may be specified in the command line, we might instead want to move the dependency rule for prog to the top. By default, make will build the first target if none are specified on the command line.

We have seen the usefulness of using macro definitions. Another improvement might be to define the list of object files as a macro. New object files are then accommodated by appending to the list of files. The final Makefile dependency specification is as follows:

```
CC = gcc
OBJECTS = x.o y.o z.o
prog: $(OBJECTS)
<tab>    $(CC) -o prog $(OBJECTS) -lcurses
x.o: def.h x.h
y.o: x.h
z.o: def.h
```

a. make depend

While suffix rules provide a convenient means of specifying how a set of files might be processed, we still rely on the dependency list to be built manually. We will demonstrate how the construction of this list might be automated.

Even if the original dependency list was manually built, it is highly likely that it must be updated as program development progresses. The list of program dependencies would then change as a result of incremental construction and new requirements. This procedure is a good case for automation.

We first present a possible skeleton of a Makefile with the make depend rule, and then provide a commentary.

```
SOURCES = list of source files
OBJECTS = list of object files
target: $(OBJECTS)
<tab> command
depend:
<tab> @echo '1,/^#.*    DO NOT DELETE THIS LINE/ w!' | ex - Makefile
<tab> @echo '# PUT NOTHING BELOW THIS LINE: make depend will remove it' >>Makefile
<tab> -grep '^#[ tab ]*include[ tab ][ tab ]*"' $(SOURCES) /dev/null | \
<tab> sed 's/\..*:#[^"]*"\([^"]*\)".*/.o:   \1/' >> Makefile

# DO NOT DELETE THIS LINE
# PUT NOTHING BELOW THIS LINE: make depend will remove it
```

Comments are introduced by a hex (#) symbol in the first column of a line, while a backslash (\) symbol at the end of the line acts as a continuation marker. This allows a long line to be written over two physical lines.

We have already mentioned that the line after a dependency specification beginning with a tab character specifies how the target of the dependency specification is to be constructed. There could be more than one command line, in which case, all are assumed to work in sequence to produce the target.

The character (@) may precede a command, with the result that the shell command is not echoed when make executes it. By default, make stops building the target if a command does not return a success exit code of 0. However, make will ignore a non-zero exit code of the command which is preceded by a minus (-) character.

Where a dependency rule does not have any dependencies and the target is never created, the associated command would always be executed. This occurs with the make depend rule, where the four command lines are always executed to rebuild the dependencies.

The make depend rule works on the Makefile itself. The first command line deletes all file dependency lines after the first warning line against its own deletion. It will thus only contain all the rules for linking object files. The second command line reinserts the second warning against deletion of user modifications.

The third and the fourth lines work to insert file dependencies. All source files, as indicated by the SOURCE variable, are searched for a #include processor directive. While /dev/null is an empty file, it ensures that grep always produces output of the form:

```
file.c: #include "def.h"
```

Output is piped to the next command line and the corresponding sed script rearranges the target file name with an .o suffix, and strips off the double quotes around the include file to produce:

```
file.o: def.h
```

The resultant output is then appended to the Makefile. This is a good example of the UNIX approach of combining a number of general-purpose programs to achieve a specific purpose.

A. 5   The gdb Debugger

The gdb debugger allows users to monitor a program by executing it under controlled conditions. It can also perform a post-mortem analysis of the core file that is produced when a program aborts.

The kernel writes out the memory contents of programs which terminated abnormally to a file named core. In some UNIX systems, their file store is littered with core files, whereas in others, none are seen. Some system administrators might initially set the maximum size of core files to zero, thus preventing core files from ever being written out by the kernel. This option is reasonable for programmers who never want to analyse their core files. Where such analysis is required, the permissible size of core files must be increased to an estimated figure which accommodates most core files.

gdb is primarily concerned with the dynamic state of a program. For example, while there might be only one definition of a function z(), gdb must represent more than one instantiation for the case of recursive calls. A function which has been called but is not yet terminated is represented by a frame. A post-mortem analysis of the core file usually requests gdb for a list of frames with the corresponding calling contexts that existed just before the program aborted. This is called a *backtrace*.

As with make, gdb is best shown by using an example. Assume that the program list.c in Listing A-1 has been compiled with the -g option:

```
1   #include <stdio.h>
2   #include <stdlib.h>
3
4   struct node {
5       int item;
6       struct node *next;
7   };
8
9   void insert(struct node **p, int x)
10  {
11      if (*p == NULL) {
12          *p = malloc(sizeof(struct node));
13          (*p)->item = x;
14          (*p)->next = NULL;
15          return;
16      }
17      insert(&(*p)->next, x);
18  }
19
20  void printList(struct node *p)
21  {
22      if (p == NULL)
23          return;
24      printf("%d\n", p->item);
25      printList(p->next);
26  }
27
28  main(int argc, char **argv)
29  {
30      struct node *first;
31
32      insert(&first, 1); insert(&first, 8);
33      insert(&first, 0); insert(&first, 9);
34      printList(first);
35      exit(0);
36  }
```

Listing A-1: Incorrect program for debugging

When executed, it terminated abnormally to produce a `core` file. `gdb` is then invoked by specifying both the program name and `core` file:

```
$ list
Bus error (core dumped)
$ gdb list core
GDB is free software and you are welcome to distribute copies of it
 under certain conditions; type "show copying" to see the
conditions.
There is absolutely no warranty for GDB; type "show warranty" for
details.
GDB 4.10.p11 (sparc-sun-solaris2.2),
Copyright 1993 Free Software Foundation, Inc...
Core was generated by `./list'.
Program terminated with signal 10, Bus error.
#0  0x107b0 in insert (p=0xdffffc22, x=1) at list.c:11
11                 if (*p == NULL) {
```

Often, analysis begins by finding out where the program terminated. This is achieved by the backtrace command `bt`. It produces output such as the following:

```
(gdb) bt
#0  0x107b0 in insert (p=0xdffffc22, x=1) at list.c:11
#1  0x10814 in insert (p=0xdffffb30, x=1) at list.c:17
#2  0x10814 in insert (p=0xdffffaac, x=1) at list.c:17
#3  0x1088c in main (argc=1, argv=0xdffffb24) at list.c:32
```

The backtrace shows that `main()` invoked `insert()`, and subsequently `insert()` calls of itself recursively for two more times before it crashed at line 11. The second argument for `insert()` shows the value of x, and that 1 is being inserted. We note that value 1 is the first item to be inserted, and as such the recursive call should not have occurred since in this instance, a first node should merely be added.

At this stage, all accessible variables in a context may be inspected via the print command `p`. We thus jump into the context associated with frame #3 via the frame command `f`, and inspect the value of `first` via the print command `p`:

```
(gdb) f 3
#3  0x1088c in main (argc=1, argv=0xdffffb24) at list.c:32
32                 insert(&first, 1); insert(&first, 8);
(gdb) p first
$1 = (struct node *) 0xdffffb2c
```

This shows that `first` contains a non-NULL uninitialised stray value, which leads to undefined areas and then to an inaccessible location. It would explain the unexpected recursive call for the `first` item in the list, and ultimately abnormal termination.

The above scenario might be too simplistic, but it shows how an autopsy might be performed on a program corpse using gdb.

The gdb debugger can also be used to confirm a diagnosis by re-executing the program. It can load and execute a fresh program, and suspend it at specified locations for the user to make appropriate changes and observe the consequences.

At this point, we will reload the `list` program but ignore the `core` file, or continue from where we left off above.

```
$ gdb list
```

We begin by setting a breakpoint – i.e. a line number or function name at which to temporarily suspend execution. It provides an opportunity to examine the context, just as before, when the context at the crash was examined. The difference with a breakpoint is that program execution may be continued. The breakpoint command is b.

```
(gdb) b main
Breakpoint 1 at 0x10878: file list.c, line 29.
```

Recall that `main()` is merely a special function which the C initialisation library calls. The `breakpoint` command specifies that execution is to stop whenever `main()` is invoked. Alternatively, the line number 32 (first line of function `main()`) could also have been specified. We could use that to re-execute the program via the command `run`.

```
(gdb) run
Starting program: /home/staff/dkiong/reports/courses/cs173/list

Breakpoint 1, main (argc=1, argv=0xdffffaf4) at list.c:32
32              insert(&first, 1); insert(&first, 8);
```

As expected, execution is temporarily suspended at the first statement of `main()`. In the context of function `main()`, we could initialise the value of `first` to NULL via the command `set`. Note that NULL in C is a macro with value 0 to signify a null pointer, and thus 0 is used instead.

```
(gdb) set first = 0
```

Execution may be resumed via the continue command c. Since only one breakpoint exists, the program executes and terminates normally. gdb may then be terminated via the command quit.

```
(gdb) c
Continuing.
1
8
0
9

Program exited normally.
(gdb) quit
$
```

A. 6   The prof Profiler

The objective of profiling is to determine the characteristics of program execution. Inefficient functions might be identified and rewritten to improve performance.

Ideally, the probes we insert into a program under investigation must gather as much information as possible. On the other hand, this must not affect its execution such that it would distort the data collected. Profiling should place little burden on CPU usage.

The -p and -pg options in gcc generate code to collect execution characteristics. The information is written into a profile file named mon.out and gmon.out respectively, just before program termination. The prof and gprof programs read these files to produce nicely formatted tables of execution characteristics.

We will first examine what statistics are collected with the -p option and how the data is processed by prof. This option generates additional code for the following purposes:

- to count the number of function activations by inserting calls to counters at the start of each function body, and

- to record the program counter at the end of time interval t.

The time attributed to function f is estimated as $t_f = t_{total} * c_f / c_{total}$, where c_{total} is the total number of program counters sampled, c_f is the number of program counters within the address space of function f, and t_{total} is the execution time of the whole program.

Since the profile file (mon.out by default) is kept as small as possible, the data is correlated with the linker symbol table in the executable program (a.out by default). From this, the time spent executing between the address of an external symbol and the next, and the average time spent per call, is printed.

Note that the results must take into account the granularity of time interval t (typically a timer clock tick) and the total execution time. Large time intervals and small execution times would produce variations in timing figures. It ultimately leads to inaccurate results.

The profiling option also requires its associated library to be included during linking[1]. It contains code that is called at the beginning of program execution to initialise counters, as well as before exit to produce the profile file of data for the particular execution run.

The trivial program waste.c, as illustrated in Listing 1-2, was profiled.

```
#define MAXLOOP 100000
int x[MAXLOOP];

a()
{
  int i, j;
  for (i=0; i<MAXLOOP; i++)
    x[i] = x[i]+3*x[i];
}

b()
{
  int i, j;
  for (i=0; i<MAXLOOP; i++)
    x[i] = x[i]+3*x[i];
  a();
}

c()
{
  int i, j;
  for (i=0; i<10; i++)
    b();
}

main()
{
  int i, j;
  for (i=0; i<MAXLOOP; i++)
    x[i] = I;
  a();
  b();
  c();
}
```

Listing A-2: Example program for profiling

---

[1] On some systems, the library is included implicitly and users need not use the -l flag as with the *curses* library.

On compiling with the -p option, and running waste, the resultant mon.out file was processed by prof to produce the statistics below:

```
$ gcc -o waste -p waste.c
$ ./waste
$ prof waste
```

%Time	Seconds	Cumsecs	#Calls	msec/call	Name
50.0	0.55	0.55	12	45.8	a
46.4	0.51	1.06	11	46.4	b
3.6	0.04	1.10	1	40.	main
0.0	0.00	1.10	1	0.	c

The Seconds and %Time columns give the absolute times and corresponding percentages spent on the function in the Name column. These figures are attributed to the function themselves and do not include those of their descendants. This is evident in the figures for function c() – even if it has a loop and performs much work, the time consumed in b() is not propagated to c(). In addition, the #Calls column gives the number of times the function is called, while the msec/call column gives the average timing per call. The latter figure can also be obtained from dividing Seconds by #Calls.

A. 7   The gprof Profiler

The profiling performed under the -pg option, and statistics reported via gprof all work in a similar fashion as -p and prof. Again, additional code is generated at compile time, and linked with the appropriate libraries.

The statistical method for obtaining timing figures is similar. The information is stored in gmon.out, and the reporting is performed by gprof. The output is however more elaborate because it takes the call graph into consideration. The statistics reported are entries in the following format, one for each function:

index	%time	self	descendents	called/total called+self called/total	parents name index children
		tp_1	tdp_1	pn_1/pnt	p_1
		...	...	...	...
		tp_k	tdp_k	pn_k/pnt	p_k
$[i]$	pt	t	td	$n+nr$	$name[i]$
		tc_1	tdc_1	cn_1/cnt_1	c_1
		...	...	...	...
		tc_m	tdc_m	cn_m/cnt_m	c_m

Figure A-3: Format of gprof *output*

name indicates the function to which the entry refers, while i represents a corresponding integer index assigned to each *name* for the purpose of quick reference. The amount of time spent in function *name* is t seconds, while td is the time spent in descendants of the function on its behalf. The number of times that *name* is invoked is given by n, while self-recursive calls are given by nr.

$tp_1...tp_k$ and $tdp_1...tdp_k$ represent the times from t and td respectively, due to calls from parent functions $p_1...p_k$. The $pn_1...pn_k$ figures give the number of times from which *name* is called from functions $p_1...p_k$. The total number of times that *name* is called by all its parents is given by pnt, which is equal to the sum of $pn_1...pn_k$.

The times $tc_1...tc_m$ and $tdc_1...tdc_m$ represent the times of descendants $c_1...c_m$, which are called from *name*. The $cn_1...cn_m$ figures give the number of times that descendants $c_1...c_m$ are called from *name*. The total number of times which functions $c_1...c_m$ are invoked are given by $cnt_1...cnt_m$ (this includes calls from other functions too).

The following statistics are obtained from profiling waste.c via the -pg option in gcc.

index	%time	self	descendents	called/total called+self called/total	parents name index children
		0.04	1.12	1/1	_start [2]
[1]	100.0	0.04	1.12	1	main [1]
		0.00	0.97	1/1	c [4]
		0.05	0.05	1/11	b [3]
		0.05	0.00	1/12	a [5]
					<spontaneous>
[2]	100.0	0.00	1.16		_start [2]
		0.04	1.12	1/1	main [1]
		0.05	0.05	1/11	main [1]
		0.49	0.48	10/11	c [4]
[3]	92.4	0.54	0.53	11	b [3]
		0.53	0.00	11/12	a [5]
		0.00	0.97	1/1	main [1]
[4]	84.0	0.00	0.97	1	c [4]
		0.49	0.48	10/11	b [3]
		0.05	0.00	1/12	main [1]
		0.53	0.00	11/12	b [3]
[5]	50.0	0.58	0.00	12	a [5]

Figure A-4: Sample gprof output

A. 8   Summary

In this appendix, useful UNIX tools for program development were discussed:

§   editor, vi and tags generator, ctags

§   compiler, gcc

§   version maintainer, make, make depend

§   debugger, gdb

§   profilers, prof and gprof

Tools are to improve the programmers' productivity. They need not be dictated or implemented by the system. The joy of working in a UNIX environment is that many different tasks are possible by using a combination of standard utilities. The possibilities are often only limited by the user's imagination.

The reader is encouraged to review additional features in the SunOS 5.x Editing Text Files and SunOS 5.x Programming Utilities.

Bibliography

For starters, the following two books by Kernighan provide a comprehensive start to learning about the UNIX operating system and the C programming language.

- Brian W. Kernighan and Rob Pike, *The UNIX Programming Environment*, Englewood Cliffs, N.J., Prentice Hall, 1984.

- Brian W. Kernighan and Dennis M. Ritchie, *The C Programming Language*, 2nd ed., Englewood Cliffs, N.J., Prentice Hall, 1988.

When elements of UNIX and C no longer seem foreign, the following book by Kernighan gives some insight to the style and philosophy of software development in a UNIX environment.

- Brian W. Kernighan and P. J. Plauger, *Software Tools*, Reading, Mass., Addison-Wesley, 1976.

The next book by Sebesta gives a broad coverage of language design and a brief introduction to language implementation. It explains why computer languages are designed the way they are.

- Robert W. Sebesta, *Concepts of Programming Languages*, 2nd ed., Redwood City, CA, Benjamin/Cummings, 1993.

The next three books give extensive coverage to the area of language implementation and compiler implementation. The Hendrix book presents the implementation of an MS-DOS compiler for a C subset. It is an interesting point that the compiler can compile itself. This book allows readers to further enhance the compiler and its libraries. The Holub book presents compiler generator tools. It gives an insight into how bigger compilers might be built. In addition, these tools are implemented in C and the reader has the opportunity to learn some C programming style. The Fischer book gives a more general overview of how a compiler might perform analysis and code synthesis phases.

- James E. Hendrix, *A Small C Compiler*, 2nd ed., Redwood City, CA, M&T Books, 1990.

- Allen I. Holub, *Compiler Design in C*, Englewood Cliffs, N.J., Prentice Hall, 1990.

- Charles N. Fischer and Richard J. LeBlanc, Jr., *Crafting a Compiler*, Menlo Park, CA, Benjamin/Cummings, 1988.

The following two books by Stevens are virtual gems for serious C programmers. The books augment the standard man pages, and contain many helpful examples to show how system and library calls are to be used.

- Richard Stevens, *UNIX Network Programming*, Englewood Cliffs, N.J., Prentice Hall, 1990.

- Richard Stevens, *Advanced Programming in the UNIX Environment*, Reading, Mass., Addison-Wesley, 1992.

Finally, the Bach and Goodheart books deal with the internals of the UNIX system. Though they are not for the faint-hearted, their readers would be enriched and enlightened.

- Maurice J. Bach, *The Design of the UNIX Operating System*, Englewood Cliffs, N.J., Prentice Hall, 1986.

- Berny Goodheart and James Cox, *The Magic Garden Explained: The Internals of UNIX System V Release 4, An Open Systems Design*, Australia, Prentice Hall of Australia, 1994.

Index

− arithmetic negation operator, 71

−− decrement operator, 7, 16, 71

− `Makefile` ignore non-zero result marker, 196

− subtraction operator, 7, 71

! logical negation operator, 7, 71

!= inequality operator, 7, 16, 71

`Makefile` comment, 196

`#define` macro definition, 8, 18, 38

`#else`, 8

`#endif`, 8

`#if` conditional compilation, 8, 38

`#ifdef` conditional compilation, 8, 39

`#ifndef` conditional compilation, 8

`#include` file inclusion, 8, 38, 192

`$<` `Makefile` macro, 195

% modulus operator, 7, 71

%= assignment operator, 72

& address-of operator, 7, 30, 71

& bitwise AND operator, 7, 72

&& logical AND operator, 7, 16, 72

&= assignment operator, 72

* indirection operator, 7, 15, 29, 71

* multiply operator, 7, 71

*= assignment operator, 72

+ addition operator, 7, 71

++ increment operator, 7, 16, 71

+= assignment operator, 7, 72

, expression list, 72

. field access operator, 7, 15, 70

`.c.o` suffix rule, 195

`.profile` initialisation, 46

/ division operator, 7, 71

`/*  ...  */` comments, 8

/= assignment operator, 72

`/dev/null`, 197

`/etc/passwd`, 141

`/tmp`, 148

`/usr/include/crypt.h`, 145

`/usr/include/curses.h`, 47, 51, 55

`/usr/include/dirent.h`, 102

`/usr/include/fcntl.h`, 94, 98

`/usr/include/pwd.h`, 142–3

`/usr/include/setjmp.h`, 160, 163

`/usr/include/signal.h`, 155, 157

`/usr/include/stdio.h`, 109–10, 115, 133, 148, 198

`/usr/include/stdlib.h`, 145, 149, 198

`/usr/include/sys/stat.h`, 94–5, 97–8, 101, 105–6

`/usr/include/sys/systeminfo.h`, 89–90

`/usr/include/sys/types.h`, 94, 98–101, 105–7, 121, 135–7

`/usr/include/sys/uio.h`, 99

`/usr/include/termios.h`, 170–1, 174

`/usr/include/time.h`, 148

`/usr/include/unistd.h`, 96–7, 99–102, 104, 107, 121, 125, 131, 135–7, 163

`/usr/lib`, 53, 192

`/usr/lib/libcurses.a`, 192

< less than operator, 7, 71

<< shift left operator, 71

<<= assignment operator, 72

<= less or equal operator, 7, 71

= assignment operator, 7, 15, 69, 72

== equality operator, 7, 15, 71

-> field access operator, 7, 15, 70

> greater than operator, 7, 71

>= greater or equal operator, 7, 71
>> shift right operator, 71
>>= assignment operator, 72
? : conditional expression, 7, 72
@ `Makefile` silent marker, 196
[] array subscript operator, 7, 65, 70
\ `Makefile` continuation character, 196
\ preprocessor continuation character, 40
\0 null character, 19, 42
\015 octal character representation, 6
\n newline character, 6, 15, 19
^ bitwise exclusive OR operator, 72
^= assignment operator, 72
{ } block, 8, 75
| bitwise inclusive OR operator, 72
| bitwise OR operator, 7
|= assignment operator, 72
|| logical OR operator, 7, 16, 72
~ one's complement operator, 7, 71

`a.out`, 26, 153, 193
`A_BLINK`, 57
`A_BOLD`, 57
`A_DIM`, 57
`A_NORMAL`, 57
`A_REVERSE`, 57
`A_STANDOUT`, 57
`A_UNDERLINE`, 57
abstraction, 33
access permissions, 95
activation record, 28
`addch()`, 48
address of variable, 31
address space, 119
`addstr()`, 48
`alarm()`, 163
ambiguities in expressions
    resolution of, 73
`append()`, 14
`argc` program argument count, 41, 120
`argv` program argument vector, 41–2, 120
array, 65
    multidimension, 65
    name of, 65

array elements
    address of, 65
array subscripts, 65
as, 191
`asctime()`, 148
`assert()`, 40
associativity, 73
asynchronous signal notification, 151
`attroff()`, 56
`attron()`, 56
`attrset()`, 57
autoindent, 189

`B0`, 180
`B50`, … `B38400`, 180
backtab, 189
backtrace, 197
`backward()`, 16
`biff`, 56
bitwise operations, 172, 174
break statement, 8, 21, 77
`BRKINT`, 178
`Buffer`, 168
    struct, 13
buffering, 108, 116

`c_cc[]`, 170, 174
`c_cflag`, 170, 172, 180
`c_iflag`, 170
`c_lflag`, 170–1, 177
`c_oflag`, 170
canonical mode, 50, 171
`CBAUD`, 180
`cbreak()`, 50, 175
`cc1`, 191
`cc1plus`, 191
`CFLAGS`, 195
char type, 6, 62
`chdir()`, 135
child process, 121
`chmod()`, 105–6
`chown()`, 105, 107

CLOCAL, 180
close(), 96
closedir(), 102
clrtobot(), 49
clrtoeol(), 49
code reusability, 33
code segment, 26
compilation, 37
compiler, 25
conditional compilation, 39
configuration control, 40
context switching, 119
continue statement, 8, 77
control constructs, 5
core, 155, 197
core dump, 124
cpp, 191
CPPFLAGS, 195
creat(), 95, 128
crypt(), 145
CS5, CS6, CS7, CS8, 173, 180
CSIZE, 173, 180
CSTOPB, 180
ctags, 190
ctime(), 148
curses, 45, 52, 167, 175, 185
cursor addressing, 46

dangling object, 30
dangling pointer, 32
data segment, 26
deadlock, 132
declarators, 64
default limb, 77
delch(), 58
delwin(), 54
dependency analysis, 194
dependency specification, 193
device driver, 167–8
directory operations, 101
dirent
    struct, 102
display(), 17, 51
disposition, 155

do-while statement, 8, 17, 76
dup(), 129
dup2(), 129
dynamic-array, 41

ECHO, 177, 183
echo(), 50
ECHOCTL, 177–8
ECHOE, 177
ECHOK, 177
ECHOKE, 177
ECHOPRT, 177
echoTo, 97
editing model, 187
EDITOR, 149
effective-group ID, 136
effective-user ID, 136–7
else part, 8, 75
encryption, 144
endpwent(), 144
endwin(), 47, 52
environ, 120
environment variables, 120
erase(), 48, 51
errno, 90–1, 155
exec family, 125–6
execl(), 125
execle(), 125
execlp(), 126
execv(), 125
execve(), 126
execvp(), 126
exit status, 122, 134
exit(), 15, 122, 124
expression
    components of, 71
    primary, 70
expression statement, 69
extern, 82

factorial, 1
fchdir(), 135

fchmod(), 106
fclose(), 110
fdopen(), 109
fflush(), 110
fgetc(), 113
fgets(), 18, 113
FILE, 108
file attributes, 105
file descriptor, 93, 127, 130
file position, 100
find, 191
flag, 171
float type, 6, 62
FLUSHO, 177–8
fopen(), 22, 109, 134
for statement, 8, 75
fork(), 121
forktrial(), 122
forward(), 16
fprintf(), 94, 111
fputc(), 110
fread(), 113
free(), 29
fscanf(), 114
fseek(), 116
fstat(), 105
ftell(), 116
function body, 79
function call, 7, 70
function declaration, 66
function definition, 7, 61, 78
function parameters, 81
fwrite(), 111

gcc, 191–2
gdb, 192, 197
general mask pattern, 172
getc(), 113
getch(), 50
getchar(), 113, 184
getegid(), 136
getenv(), 149
geteuid(), 136
getgid(), 135

getpass(), 145
getpid(), 135
getppid(), 135
getpwent(), 144
getpwnam(), 142, 144, 165
getpwuid(), 142
gets(), 113
getuid(), 135
getw(), 113
gmon.out, 203
gmtime(), 148
goto statement, 78, 158
gprof, 192, 201, 203
group ID, 135, 137

heap allocator, 29
heap pool, 33
high-level languages, 4
home(), 16
HUPCL, 180

ICANON, 171, 176–7, 183
ICRNL, 179
identify, 143
IEXTEN, 176–7
if statement, 8, 16
if-else statement, 74
IGNBRK, 178
IGNCR, 179
IGNPAR, 178
IMAXBEL, 179
indentation, 189
independent compilation, 5, 84
initialisation, 27
initscr(), 47, 52
INLCR, 179
inode, 103–4
input
    preprocessing of, 169
insch(), 58
int type, 6, 62
intercharacter timer, 181

interrupt key, 151
intro(2) manual page, 90
ISIG, 176–7
IUCLC, 179
IXANY, 179
IXOFF, 179
IXON, 176, 179

key bindings, 174–5, 183
KEY_DOWN, 55
KEY_LEFT, 55
KEY_RIGHT, 55
KEY_UP, 55
keypad(), 55
kill, 151–3

-lcurses, 53, 192
ld, 191
less, 130, 149
library, 37
Line
    struct, 13
line characteristics, 169
line editing, 58
line-number, 189
link
    file, 104
link(), 105
linker, 5, 37, 53
literal
    character, 6
    decimal, 6
    floating point, 6
    octal, 6
local terminal discipline, 169
localtime(), 148
login, 138
longjmp(), 160
ls, 106
lseek(), 100
lvalue, 72

main(), 21, 37, 52
make, 193
make depend, 196
Makefile, 195
malloc(), 15, 19, 29
man pages, 12
manual pages, 88
map, 187
mask, 172
matching delimiters, 188
MIN, 181, 184
mkdir(), 101
module, 33
    example of, 34
mon.out, 201
move(), 48, 51
multi-user, 119

newwin(), 54
nocbreak(), 50
noecho(), 50
non-blocking read, 184
non-canonical-mode, 181
non-local branches, 159
NULL, 12–3, 15, 18, 30–1, 102, 109–10, 123,
    125, 134
null return statement, 79

O_APPEND, 98
O_CREAT, 98
O_EXCL, 99
O_RDONLY, 98
O_RDWR, 98
O_TRUNC, 99
O_WRONLY, 98
OCRNL, 179
OFDEL, 180
OFILL, 180
OLCUC, 179
ONLCR, 179
ONLRET, 179
ONOCR, 179

open(), 98, 128
opendir(), 102
operating system, 87
OPOST, 179
optimisation, 49
output
    postprocessing of, 169

pagination, 130
PARENB, 180
parent process, 121
PAREXT, 180
PARMRK, 178
PARODD, 180
Pascal, 1
pass-by-reference, 80
pass-by-value, 79
passwd
    struct, 142, 144
password, 144
password file, 141
password validation, 145
pattern mask, 171
pclose(), 134
PENDIN, 177–8
pine, 149
pipe, 40, 130
pipe(), 131
pointer variable, 64
polling, 151
popen(), 134
precedence, 67, 73
preprocessor directives, 38
printf(), 17, 48, 94, 111
printw(), 48, 51
process ID, 127, 135
process number, 121
process scheduler, 122
prof, 192, 201
program arguments, 41
ps, 106, 152
pts, 185
public names, 5
putc(), 110

putchar(), 110, 184
putenv(), 149
puts(), 111
putw(), 110
pw_dir, 142
pw_gecos, 142
pw_gid, 142
pw_name, 142
pw_passwd, 142
pw_shell, 142
pw_uid, 142

read(), 99, 108, 184
readCommandsAndInterpret(), 20, 52
readdir(), 102
readFile(), 18
recursive function, 27
redirection
    of input/output, 127
    of output, 130
redraw(), 56
re-entrant, 165
refresh(), 49, 52, 55
register, 83
report_err(), 91, 94
return address, 28
return statement, 8, 79
rmdir(), 101
run-time library, 37
run-time organisation, 25

S_IRGRP, 95
S_IROTH, 95
S_IRUSR, 95
S_IRWXG, 95
S_IRWXO, 95
S_IRWXU, 95
S_IWGRP, 95
S_IWOTH, 95
S_IWUSR, 95
S_IXGRP, 95
S_IXOTH, 95

S_IXUSR, 95
sbrk(), 29
scanf(), 114
screen attributes, 46
sed, 197
SEEK_CUR, 100
SEEK_END, 100
SEEK_SET, 100
sendmail, 148
setegid(), 137
seteuid(), 137
setgid(), 137–8
setjmp(), 160
setpwent(), 144
setuid, 136–137
setuid(), 137–8
shiftwidth, 189
short-circuit, 7
showmatch, 188
SI_HOSTNAME, 90
SI_SET_HOSTNAME, 90
side-effect, 69
SIG_DFL, 155
SIG_ERR, 155
SIG_IGN, 155
SIGABRT, 153
SIGALRM, 154, 163–4
SIGBUS, 154
SIGCHLD, 154
SIGEMT, 154
SIGFPE, 154
SIGHUP, 153
SIGILL, 153
SIGINT, 153, 158, 175–7
SIGKILL, 154, 158
siglongjmp(), 163
signal, 124
    interrupt, 123
    kill, 123
    responding to a, 155
signal handler
    installing a, 156
signal(), 155
SIGPIPE, 154
SIGQUIT, 153, 158, 175, 177

SIGSEGV, 154
sigset(), 157
sigsetjmp(), 163
SIGSYS, 154
SIGTERM, 154
SIGTRAP, 153
SIGTSTP, 175, 177
SIGUSR1, 154
SIGUSR2, 154
SIGWINCH, 154
sizeof(), 8, 15, 65, 71
specific mask pattern, 172
sprintf(), 111
sscanf(), 114
st_atime, 106
st_ctime, 106
st_gid, 106
st_mode, 106
st_mtime, 106
st_nlink, 106
st_size, 106
st_uid, 106
stack segment, 26
standend(), 48, 52, 56
standout(), 48, 52, 56
stat
    struct, 105
stat(), 105
static, 83
stderr, 94
STDERR_FILENO, 94, 128
stdin, 108
STDIN_FILENO, 94, 128
stdio, 108, 116
stdio conversion specification
    %%, 112, 114
    %[...], 115
    %c, 112, 115
    %d, 17, 111, 114
    %e, 112
    %f, 112, 115
    %g, 112
    %i, 111, 114
    %o, 111, 114
    %s, 17, 112, 115

stdio conversion specification (*cont*)
    %u, 111, 114
    %x, 111, 114
stdio.h, 12
stdlib.h, 12
STDOUT_FILENO, 94, 128
stdscr, 54
storage allocation, 5
storage requirements, 5
strcpy(), 19–20
streams, 108
struct, 7, 62
stty, 167, 175, 185
su, 138
suffix rule, 195
switch statement, 8, 21, 77
sys_errlist, 90–1
sys_nerr, 91
sysinfo(), 89

tab, 188
tabstop, 188
tags file, 190
tcgetattr(), 170
tcputattr(), 170
TCSADRAIN, 170
TCSAFLUSH, 170
TCSANOW, 170
temporary files, 148
TERM environment variable, 46
termcap, 45
terminfo(4) manual page, 55
termio, 185
termios, 171–2, 180, 183, 185
    struct, 170
TIME, 181, 184
time slice, 119
time_t, 146
timeout, 181
tm
    struct, 146
tm_hour, 147
tm_isdst, 147
tm_mday, 147

tm_min, 147
tm_mon, 147
tm_sec, 147
tm_wday, 147
tm_yday, 147
tm_year, 147
tmpfile(), 148, 165
tmpnam(), 148
TOSTOP, 177
touchwin(), 56
type casting, 8, 71, 81
type definitions, 5
type specifiers, 62
typedef, 68

union, 6, 63
unlink(), 102
user ID, 135, 137

variable
    global, 27
    heap, 28
    local, 27
variable definition, 61–2
VDISCARD, 176–7
VDSUSP, 175
vector, 125
VEOF, 176
VERASE, 176
vi, 50, 187
VINTR, 174–5
VKILL, 176
VLNEXT, 176–7
VMIN, 176
Von Neumann, 2–3
Von Neumann model, 2
VQUIT, 175
VREPRINT, 176–7
VSTART, 176
VSTOP, 176
VSUSP, 175
VTIME, 176

VWERASE, 176–7

waddch(), 54
waddstr(), 54
wait(), 122–3
wclrtobot(), 54
wclrtoeol(), 54
werase(), 54

wgetch(), 54
while statement, 8, 16, 75
WINDOW, 54
wmove(), 54
wprintw(), 54
wrefresh(), 54
write(), 96, 108, 184
wstandend(), 54
wstandout(), 54
WSTOPFLG, 124